DANNY NICHOLSON

MY OWN
backyard

Ann —

God Bless you!

For the Dreams of Children,

Danny Nicholson

DANNY NICHOLSON

MY OWN, backyard

Explore "My Own Backyard" .... then discover yours.

In his autobiographical book, "My Own Backyard," Danny Nicholson explores the landscape of his own backyard through stories about his father, poems about his children, and songs about family, faith and friends.

In essence, this book reveals that his story is not his own. It transcends the boundaries of geographical locations, suggesting that life is not so much where we are but who we are.

From chapter one:
"Geographical boundaries separate backyards, but the memories we make in them create a sameness and familiarity that renders the distance between them non-existent. In other words, backyards are set apart by their location, but they are made of the same stuff. Or even better, we are made of the same stuff."

This book reveals that our "sameness" is greater than our differences. You won't be surprised to find scenes from your own backyard weaved within these pages. Nicholson's stories, poems, and songs of laughter and tears, darkness and light, faith and love, inextricably link us to each other as human beings, and give us a divine reason to hope for a better tomorrow.

As Dorothy says in the *Wizard of Oz*, "...if I ever go looking for my heart's desire again, I won't look any further than my own backyard. Because if it isn't there I never really lost it to begin with."

 COURIER PUBLISHING

Greenville, South Carolina
baptistcourier.com

Danny Nicholson
My Own Backyard
109 Jamison Street North
Greenwood, S.C. 29646

dannynicholson.com

Ordering Information:
Special discounts are available on quantity purchases by corporations,
associations, and others. For details, contact the author at the address above.

Hardcover ISBN #978-0-9905788-0-2
Softcover ISBN #978-1-940645-60-5

Press date, December 2018

Cover art and art direction:
SUSANNE S. CATE ᔕ scatedesign@gmail.com
DANDRIDGE, TENNESSEE

Printed in the United States of America

"

I have traveled all over the world, and have met hundreds of thousands of people. Danny Nicholson stands alone among those people. I have stood in his backyard (literally where he lives today) and I have stood with him on many occasions in his allegorical backyard as he describes in this book. Danny is one of the most authentic, deeply caring human beings I have ever met! He is a genuine "pilgrim" whose heart and journey have always been in the right direction. This book takes you inside that "journey" and gives you a glimpse of what it means to say "Yes" to life and to discover what really matters, and in the end, what's most important! Some people say you should plant a garden in your backyard, Danny says there's already one there, go find it!

GENE COTTON
Singer/Songwriter
Nashville, Tennessee

～ ～ ～

The volume you hold in your hand is a treasure because the man who wrote it is a treasure. Anyone who has the great fortune to know Danny Nicholson will agree. The acknowledgements in this volume are long - longer than normal. That's because Danny has a heart full of love and appreciation. Not only for his backyard and his stories and his songs but people. Especially people. Enjoy this treasure from the heart of Danny.

RUTH GRAHAM
Ruth Graham Ministries

～ ～ ～

Danny is a singer, a poet, a storyteller. To read Danny is to feel that beautiful heart beating, for home, to be rocked in the cradle of your own childhood memories. He is our brother, our fellow pilgrim on the way. Looking for a way home to your memories? Why not take a stroll through "My Own Backyard" with Danny and remember what life and love are all about!!

J. RANDALL O'BRIEN
President, Carson-Newman University

"

DEDICATION

It has taken me a lifetime to write this book.

Because of that, a lifetime of gratitude is appropriate.

First and foremost, I want to thank my mom and dad, Billy and Mary Nicholson, for adopting me and giving me "My Own Backyard" in April, 1962. Your unconditional love and unwavering support built the foundation for my life, my faith, and any contribution I made in the lives of others. My dreams came true because of you.

My wife Debra and two sons, Bryson and Taylor, have given me a family. Debra has been my rock, my best friend, and my devoted partner in ministry and life. "Forever." She is the best wife and mother one could ever dream of having and spend one's life with. My sons are the only real "blood" I have ever known. Your wonderful lives in music and "good hearts" have made me truly proud as a father. Remember the final chapter was written for my grandchildren. You will never know how much I truly love you. Thanks to our dogs Maggie, Summer, Marley, and Tyson for showing our family the meaning of unconditional love.

My hero, mentor, and friend, Gene Cotton, listened to my heart's desire through a letter in 1986 and took me under his wing to change my life through his inspiring example and selfless service. His music, production and recording of my music in his home, and invitation to surrender my songs to a greater cause than myself and commercial success has been a constant guiding light in my vocation, creative offerings and ministry.

Nicaragua...
Legacy Road...
I've Seen a Picture...
The Hymn of Resurrection...
The Circle Goes on...

The God-Mother of my children, Barbara "Binky" Mead, has been a constant encouragement and motivating force behind my determination to make a difference. Her constant words of affirmation and enduring support showed me what it truly meant to love without ever asking for anything in return. The leaves are forever green...

My "big brother" Brooks Shumake has been as close as family since playing basketball in high school. I shall never forget the day you came over during Christmas holidays and listened to my music. The nights we spent between "concrete and heaven" in Botany Woods were the best days I have ever known. Your Reds championship ring remains one of the greatest gifts of my life.

Thanks to Kevin Jones for being my life long partner and friend in ministry. The night you drove up in the red CRX and surrendered your life and music was a gift to me. The writing of "Judgement of the Colors" was a "holy" moment. Thanks for carrying me through the dark days. I will never forget it. There will always be just... One More.

Jeff Francisco is a lifelong friend who I thank God for every day. From the first night on the lake in Awanita Valley to your long standing management and support of Heart of Love ministries through the years, you proved to be a faithful servant and loyal friend. Your encouragement, wise counsel, and perfect handwritten letters have fueled my desire to be true to myself and God. The last picture in this book is symbolic in honoring our journey together.

The years I spent with Randall O'Brien at Carson-Newman University were some of the best I've ever known. The late nights of playing guitars, laughing, and listening to your wise counsel will never be forgotten. Our visit "up the mountain" with Ruth Graham to meet her dad was one of the "holy moments" of my entire life. Don't forget the picture you took with me and Larry Bird!! "The Forgiveness Initiative" at Connie Maxwell was the culmination of God's work in our friendship and ministry together.

The times I had the honor of traveling with James B. Edwards were great experiences. From hearing Ronald Reagan stories to eating dinner at the Peninsula Grill in Charleston, Jim and Anne were examples of greatness and humility. He gave to me a leadership example to follow for the rest of my life. I will never forget my last moments with him on the porch overlooking the water in Mount Pleasant.

I want to thank Ruth Graham for dropping by Carson-Newman University in Jefferson City, Tennessee. It has been a humble privilege to experience her precious friendship and powerful example. One of the most "holy moments" of my life was the day we went to Montreat, North Carolina and visited her father, Billy Graham.

Throughout my high school and college years, my coaches and teammates were important in molding and shaping my dreams, character, and life's purpose. No words can hold their impact on my life.

Thanks to my coaches: Charlie Burry, Paul Rogers, Marc Embler, and Thad Talley.

Special thanks to Coach Jim and Betty Settle for attending every meaningful moment of my life. My respect and appreciation for your constant presence in my life is immeasurable. Also thanks to my teammates: Kenny Kinect, Pete Williams, Irving Batten, Al Dunn, and Glen Gorton.

Thanks to Pete Williams for being the best college roommate ever. Also, for introducing me to Glen, Jeff, and playing "The Cross He Gave to Me" for the first time.

Glen Gorton remains the greatest spiritual mentor in my life. The trophy you gave me after you won the mile race at Furman University still sits on my desk as a reminder of your example and impact on my life.

The people of my hometown Hartsville were meaningful in giving me a genuine sense of love, care, and spiritual support.

Thanks to Rev. Bill Bouknight for giving me strong spiritual guidance during my teen years and for conducting my father's funeral service.

Thanks to Mark Daniel for being the first friend to share his love of God on Wilson Drive late one night while we were camping out in the clubhouse. I will never forget the first year in Charleston!!

Thanks to Randy Twitty for all the rides to basketball practice with loud music and gatorade gum. You are a Godly man and I will always love and respect you.

I also want to thank my West Hartsville Baptist Church and St. Lukes Methodist Church families for your support through the years. Thanks to Bev Kennedy for baptizing my sons and Walt Peterson for remaining steadfast in the left hand corner!!

Jamie Morphis and Lucy Brown (Beth and Bo) were my hometown family and friends when I returned to Hartsville. The thanksgiving lunches delivered to Johnny, Rotary projects, "Making a Difference" Educational Foundation, Legacy Road, and your many gifts and surprise visits hold a very special place in my heart. I still sit in the chair you gave me in Myrtle Beach for my USC graduation.

Special thanks to Doc and Izzie Morphis for the honor of holding so many wonderful events in "their own backyard."

Heart of Love Ministries was a family. For over 15 years, we travelled in Hertz-Penske trucks and played music ministering to thousands of young people across the southeast. "Entertaining the heart with an uncompromising stand of commitment" was a way of life.

Mike and Tammi Gunter, Steve and Shan Johnson, Matthew Buckner, Mick Purdy, Kevin and Betty Jones, Pam and Jimmy Sanders, Allen Dykstra, Allison Barteet, Chuck Wilson, Dave and Laurie Hix, Brian Turner, Brooks Shumake, Pete Williams, Stephen Edwards, Darryl Horne, and Jake Gulledge were dedicated to a mission bigger than themselves.

Jim Daniels and Frank Bush were two strong examples of leadership and friendship, a gift to me during my days at Coker College. Jim Daniels provided a lasting example of integrity and taught me that one's values and principles stand above the approval of men. Frank Bush taught me everything I know about fundraising. From the first time dancing on the table in Frankie's art class to our many CASE adventures, Frank was a mentor and friend that made life both fun and meaningful. The Fort picture will go down as one of the greatest pranks of all time!

Our family still calls 26 Olde Canal Loop in Pawley's Island home. During my time on the coast, three mentors and friends made a lasting impact.

Jim Creel and I spent many "holy" lunches together and shared a quality of fellowship that stands out in my mind and heart. Thanks Jim for showing up at my father's funeral. I will never forget that moment!!

Also, thanks to Pete and Betsy Barr for being there for me and making West Virginia feel like Home.

Carl Falk made a lasting contribution by sharing many meaningful words of wisdom and by exemplifying his rock solid example of selfless service to Christ. Our dinner with the Edwards in Charleston, breakfast meetings at Eggs Up Grill, and the James Taylor concert experience are lasting memories. You are a man after God's own heart.

CASE (Council for Advancement and Support of Education) was 25 years of friendships and stories that made my life richer and more meaningful. Libba Andrews and Tina Kauffmann were the creators of "Table 7" at Tulane University in New Orleans and the reason the song "From Here" was written. Thank you for lifetime friendships that stand the test of time. Believe!!

Also, special thanks to Rita Bornstein and Freeman Hrabowski who shaped my understanding of leadership and fundraising beyond words. Their example changed my life. I will never forget the honor of Rita presenting me the Grezebach Award in Chicago and Freeman allowing me to join him on top of the tenth floor overlooking Baltimore. Freeman's powerful leadership example encouraged me to finish "my own story" at Connie Maxwell Children's Home. Holdfast to Dreams!!

Lastly, thanks to my Connie Maxwell family for welcoming me home.

I

Yea, the sparrow hath found an house,
and the swallow a nest for herself,
where she may lay her young,
even thine altars, O LORD of hosts,
my King, and my God.
PSALM 84:3, NIV

Entering my old driveway, my heart beats faster and my emotions swell within me. The feeling builds like it does right before a concert or the opening of a baseball game. The excitement pulls me through the old steel gate entrance which signals a sense of nostalgia and reverence. And there a dozen memories open their arms and celebrate my arrival: The old pecan tree, the light on the back porch, my mother's face in the kitchen window. As I turn the car off, I sit in silence, almost scared to disturb the music and poetry of memories that reveal themselves in the scrapbook of my mind and heart. I'm home again – safe in the cradle of my own backyard.

This experience never fails to move me. It never weakens; only growing stronger as the years unfold. It reminds me of an old time drive-in where the same old movies are showing every night. Even so, I sit and wait for the sun to set and the movie to begin. Spellbound and captured by the flickering images of 8 millimeter black and white, I watch my life unfold.

I see a young boy lying on the ground on a warm spring day with a basketball as a pillow. He's dreaming about the day he would hit the last shot to win the high school game. The same kid stares into the starry autumn night and asked God how far away heaven is behind the soft glowing radiance of the moon. The next moment, I see freshly washed shirts waving on the clothesline like tall lanky men dancing in a parade. I smell freshly cut grass and then I hear the sound of a leather baseball against a wooden bat. My dad's workshop stands as a monument in the left hand corner of the yard. The old cement basketball court is there, and the picnic table where several teenage boys sliced open a ripened watermelon to top off a hot summer day.

There are so many memories I fail to see them all, but I remember there were go-carts racing around in circles, good friends splashing in a pool, a game of kick the can, the distant sound of the six o'clock whistle, and young boys chattering about what Santa Claus brought them on Christmas morning.

Sometimes it all seems like a dream. But then I look in the mirror and realize these are the memories that made me who I am. And when I share with others about these experiences, from this most cherished place, they act as if they understand. It's like they recognize a part of themselves in my own backyard. I believe them. Geographical boundaries separate backyards, but the memories we make in them create a sameness and familiarity that renders the distance between them non-existent. In other words, backyards are set apart by their location, but they are made of the same stuff. Or even better, we are made of the same stuff.

That young boy was not just playing basketball; he was learning how to dream. As he stared into the night, he was not talking to himself, he was talking to God. He was beginning to grow and understand that faith is not knowing all the answers, but asking God questions and not being afraid to say, "I don't know." The sight of freshly washed clothes on the line and smell of newly cut grass still to this day stand as reminders of how much we treasure the simple things. The friends, games, and familiar sounds are woven together like that old throw blanket that's still draped across the end of the couch and serves to warm us when we find ourselves cold and shaking in a lost and lonely world. For sure, backyards are different, but the dreams, faith, and simple ordinary treasures of home remain the same. Always have been, always will be. Sometimes I think we'd trade all that we own to touch these ordinary splendors of home.

That's why I wanted to write about my own backyard. You see, I believe that backyards and hearts are much the same. We may be different people – different colors, different religions, different values - but we experience love, tears, broken hearts, and laughter much the same.

Our likeness is stronger than our differences, and as long as this is the case, there is a reason to find our connecting places and learn from them. Perhaps this is the very exercise that could bring us closer together. I believe that my backyard, my heart, is that connecting place. And as I share these scribbled-down thoughts from a napkin, sacred stories, humble prayers, and simple songs, it is my prayer that they will encourage you to remember with awe and wonder where you came from and inspire you with boldness and strength to envision where you are going.

Playing yardball. Hartsville, South Carolina, 1996.

2

GOD MADE THE STARS

But Lift up your eyes and look to the heavens: Who created all these?
He who brings out the starry host one by one and calls forth each of them by name.
Because of his great power and mighty strength, not one of them is missing.
ISAIAH 40:26, NIV

"God Made the Stars" is one of my favorite stories, and I am sure it will be until the day I die. It was given to me late one summer evening by my son, Taylor, who was nearly four at the time.

It happened one night after we returned from a family trip. Every time we came home after dark, I would carry Taylor in my arms down the road for a walk. The stars were scattered in the sky, and being a songwriter, I would begin to sing a song that I made up. It went like this:

> *God made the stars for you and me*
> *God made the stars for us to see*
> *God made the stars for you and me*
> *God made the stars for Taylor and Daddy.*

One night, as I finished singing, Taylor looked into my eyes as only a child can and said, "Daddy, where is God?"

It was such a surprise to me. Finally, I looked back at him and said, "Taylor, God is not in the stars, far away. Son, God is in your heart."

He seemed a little bored with my answer and laid his head back down on my shoulder. Later that week, I wanted to test Taylor and see what he would say. I asked him, "Taylor, where is God?"

He paused and said, "He's in your heart." Then he said something I will never forget. "Daddy, how does God come out?"

Human beings have been asking that question since the beginning of time. But in that moment the answer came to me...the deepest theology in the world. I said, "Taylor, God comes out when I love you and when you love me. God comes out when we love."

I always heard that HEAVEN
Was just beyond the moon
Made of LACE and priceless treasures
Golden Gates and Silver Spoons

And just beyond the rainbow
~~there's~~ Are castles in ~~the sky~~ for my self

With columns made of purest pearl
And lined with silver shelfs

That ~~will~~ hold the many treasures
From the victories that I've won

And we'll sit back and laugh about
the suffering that we've done

And we'll guard our fine ~~n~~ fishn
on dreams while we sleep
in a long awaited paradise with
No more rules to keep

(Chorus)

Original handwritten
poem "Silver Spoon."

18

3

SILVER SPOON

The kingdom of heaven is like treasure hidden in a field.
When a man found it, he hid it again, and then in his joy went
and sold all he had and bought that field.
Again, the kingdom of heaven is like a merchant looking for fine pearls.
When he found one of great value, he went away and sold
everything he had and bought it.
MATTHEW 13:44-46, NIV

Where is Heaven?

It is a question that has been asked a million times since the beginning of world. Is there a place we go when we die? And if there is, what does it look like? Is it somewhere way beyond the clouds? All of these questions just leave us with more questions, and soon the mind gets bogged down in what cannot be seen or touched. I must admit, since I am human, it is a leap of faith that brings me to a place where all my understanding surrenders to the reality of a place called heaven.

I remember when I was a young child my family would visit my grandparents during Christmas. My step grandfather was a kind and gentle man. He had worked in the construction business for years and he operated as a foreman while building the Carolina Coliseum at the University of South Carolina. I remember that because I was a big Gamecock basketball fan and I was proud of the fact that my granddad helped build the place where all my heroes played basketball.

I will never forget one time when we arrived at my grandparents' home, I saw a basketball goal that had been constructed just for me. It was my granddad's way of showing me he cared and that he could relate to the world of his eight-year-old grandson. Though he never really said it, I knew my granddad loved me.

My grandfather showed his love for me in unique ways; like the time he took me to a Carolina Gamecock basketball game. I was ten years old. It was the first ball game where I actually saw my hero, John Roche, in person. I loved

John Roche so much that I once took his picture to the barber shop and asked to have my hair cut just like his! My granddad somehow understood the dreams of a kid, and as I reflect, he wanted to make this a night to remember. Because he had worked on the construction of the coliseum, he had made friendships with many of the people who surrounded the basketball program at USC, I guess you could say he had an inside track when it came to "opening doors."

At half time, he said, "Follow me, I have something I want to show you." We walked down the aisle of the seats, onto the floor, and through the busyness of all the people. When we stopped, he said, "Danny, I want you to meet someone." I looked up and heard him say, "This is John Roche." My heart started beating and I felt like I was in a dream. There before my very eyes was my hero, the player I looked up to and admired. Out of the corner of my eye I could see my granddad smiling from ear to ear. He loved it as much as I did.

When my grandfather retired from construction, he bought 40 acres of farmland in Clover, South Carolina. It was his dream to build a home for he and my grandmother so they could spend their golden years away from the "rat race." One day, when we visited at Christmas, we walked every inch of that land together. I marveled at the trees, streams, animals and beautiful landscapes. But most of all, I was captivated by the silence and solitude that permeated the forest. I loved that farm and had a vision of one day being able to ride a horse on that land. In fact, I told my granddad I would love to have a horse. It was a magical place, but more than the place, it was the love and security of my granddad that touched my heart. Even though we walked in silence, I knew he loved me and I loved him.

When I was 12 years old, I was alone in my home one day when the telephone rang. It was my grandmother. She was hysterically screaming, "Your grandfather is dying. His tractor has turned over and crushed him. I need help." I immediately called my mother. I remember feeling scared and confused about what was happening. We received the word a little later that he had died.

I found out later that he had made an appointment to go and pick up a gift for me. It was the horse I had asked him for. Unfortunately, that never happened but it reminded me of his desire to make the farmland a place that I would love and share with him. As I reflect on the old farm, I know it wasn't so much the place that I loved. It was his love for me, his desire to make me happy and give me experiences a little boy only dreams of that made my visits so memorable. It was my granddad, not the place.

I think that story is a good analogy of Heaven. From a Christian perspective, the Bible talks about streets of gold and mansions. I know it's a beautiful place, but does it really matter? Is that what I am truly looking for? Is that the reason I want to go?

Heaven is like everything else to us human beings. We take things God has made for His purposes and use them for our purposes. For instance, sex. I know... I know what you're thinking: How can I relate a word like sex to Heaven? That is the very point. We make words out to be what we want them to be and not what they truly are. Sex was made by God for two people to become one. It is an act of worship which culminates in the birth of a child. It has a purpose and brings us pleasure in the process. Its purpose is not a dirty one. Sex has been made dirty by the way man has used it to please himself. It was more accurately created by God for worship, but just like Heaven, we have made it mean something that pleases ourselves. Any time we try to change the reason something was made for God's pleasure into our pleasure, we as humans make a grave mistake.

If you ask people, "Where is Heaven?" or, "What is Heaven?" you will be amazed at the answers you will hear. I have heard everything from vacations to something close to Disney World. I truly believe that some folks think Heaven is a place where you go to fish or live in a mansion for the rest of eternity. But that is not the concept. The right source of information for the Christian would be the words that Jesus used for Heaven. When asked,"Where is the Kingdom of Heaven?" Jesus answered, "It is within you." He also said, "The Kingdom of Heaven is like a pearl that a businessman found and after finding it; he went and sold everything he owned and bought that one pearl." The question is, "What is that pearl?" Is it a place like Disney World or a fishing resort? I think not. The Pearl is Jesus. If you want to go to Heaven for any other reason than Jesus, I am not sure you will go at all. The way I read it... Heaven is Jesus and if you don't embrace His love and presence here on earth; then I imagine you will be bored in Heaven.

It's just like it was with my granddad. I didn't want to go to visit because of the beautiful farmland or the horse. It wasn't even the fact that he introduced me to famous people. It was the way I felt when I was with him, the love and security he offered me as a young child looking for someone to depend on and trust. Heaven is a place; a person; a purpose.

SILVER SPOON

I always thought that Heaven
Was just beyond the moon,
Made of lace and priceless treasures,
Golden gates and silver spoons,
And just beyond the Rainbow
There's a castle for myself,
With columns made of purest pearl
And lined with silver shelves.
They hold my many trophies
From the victories I've won,
And there I won't have to talk about
All the crying that I've done.
I'll spend my time a fishing
Or dreaming while I sleep,
In a long awaited paradise
There will be no more rules to keep.

I can't wait for Heaven
I wish that I could die,
And finally go to that vacation in the sky.
But it's getting kind of hard to sit alone and cry
I wish I could tell this world goodbye

It's getting hard... hard for me to bear,
To leave me in this lonely world
Sometimes it seems unfair.
When You have made me such a home,
And there's a million starving people
But they don't understand,
The talk within this steeple
The plan for mortal man.
Sometimes I think about them

And it makes me want to cry,
But then I just remember
Very soon I'll say goodbye.

Well my day it finally came
And I smiled as I went home,
He opened up the pearly gates
And I stood before the throne.
He handed me a Silver Spoon
And He opened up a door,
And there before my very eyes
Were a million maybe more,
Of all the starving people
He commanded us to feed,
And those who love the least of these
Will spend Heaven here with Me.

Now I love the people
That once just made me cry
Because I finally told myself goodbye.

4

THE TREE OF LIFE

That person is like a tree planted by streams of water,
which yields its fruit in season and whose leaf does not whither—
whatever they do prospers.
PSALMS 1:3, NIV

PRETEND THAT LIFE IS NOTHING BUT A TREE
AND IT'S GROWING CONSTANTLY.
YOUR ONLY RESPONSIBILITY IS TO STAND STRONG
AND GROW IN PEACE.

As I started the encore song for my final set, the crowd erupted and I felt the connection between their hearts and mine. As I finished the song and walked off stage, I knew I had found myself. I was exactly where I belonged. But as I walked down the long, dark corridor back to my dressing room, I saw a myriad of memories flash across the movie screen within my mind. It had been a long, hard road, and the moment transported me back to my childhood. There I stood before that old tree in my backyard - the place where I was born.

The tree my daddy had planted so many years ago was my friend. In the summer, it provided shade to sit under. In the fall, it was painted with colorful leaves that danced in the wind. In the spring, it turned green and I would climb to its highest place and hide from the world. It was a tree house, a high pole that held the sail for my pirate ship. It was a song when the wind blew through the limbs and leaves. It was my constant companion, encouraging me to think and say all that was on my heart and mind. It listened and provided a place of solitude for my imagination and the yearnings of my soul. At night it held the moon in its hand. In the day it held the treehouse in which my friends and I played card games and spin the bottle with the girls in the neighborhood. It was always there.

As I grew older, it provided shade near the old basketball court where we would slice a watermelon open after a hard fought battle. And it even served as a place of silence where I figured out all the hard times in high school.

It was hard to say goodbye to my old friend when I left for college because no one else knew me like the dancing giant in my backyard. I remember watching it in my rear view mirror when I drove away. I swear I heard it crying when I pulled out the driveway, its limbs waving goodbye in the wind. The swing hanging from the lowest limb was rocking to and fro as I took my last glimpse over my shoulder.

To my surprise, the old tree was gone when I came back for Christmas break. My dad had made a decision to cut it down. "The old tree was dying," he said. There was a sadness in his heart that mimicked the pain I felt over the empty yard.

"Who cut the tree down dad?" I asked. Mr. Johnson, the carpenter from down the street. The old man said that he thought the tree would be useful for a couple of projects he had in mind."

The next day I walked down to Mr. Johnson's home and knocked on his door. He answered as politely and gently as he always had and said, "May I help you, son?"

"Yes, sir" I said. "My dad said you cut down the old tree in my backyard, and I have come to see what you did with her." He paused and said, "She was good for a few pieces of furniture." He showed me a chair and table that he had created. Then he pointed to the corner of his room where a beautiful guitar sat on a stand. "The guitar was carved out of the heart of the tree. It was the perfect size for the prize piece - a beautifully constructed instrument."

I stared at the workmanship of my childhood dreams. During that moment of silence, I think the old man heard everything that was being said in my heart. He walked across the room and picked up the guitar. Then he did something that I will never forget. He handed it to me. "This is for you, my son." I gasped, "For me?"

"Yes," he said. "The guitar is a gift to you."

I could tell he understood what this old tree meant to me and he wanted me to hold the cradle of my childhood memories in my hands.

I will never forget that moment. I began to play around with the guitar that evening and the sounds that came out of it were sweeter than anything I had ever heard in my life. The sounds gave me that same soothing feeling I had when I was a young boy in the tree. In fact, I could almost hear the wind blowing across my backyard when I played the chords. I did not put it down for the rest of my Christmas break. When I returned to college, I found a classmate who showed me how to play. I played night and day, and soon the sounds started to remind me of all the memories of my younger days. I scribbled down on a piece of paper these images in my mind and heart. Before long, my friends and family began to ask me to sing these songs for parties and gatherings, and it never ceased to amaze me how many people said they felt the same way I did. They cried and laughed when I sang. It made me feel like I was in my backyard with my old friend every time I played. Soon I was recording my songs to give to others. A few years later, I was standing in front of thousands, singing, for the most part, about my childhood dreams.

Sometimes I wonder, when I am on stage, if the old tree is still not talking to me about those wonderful moments in the summer when I rested under her branches. It seems everyone has a tree in their backyard, a place where their memories speak to them about days gone by. I think that which holds our memories also holds our future, or at least holds the substance of all that we are and all that we become. In my case, the tree held and unveiled all that I longed for in my life. It was a place to remember all that I hold dear; a place for others to remember the same things. It begs me to ask: "Is everyone looking for a way back to their childhood memories? Are all the sounds, stories, songs, and poems trying to recapture what once was innocent and white as snow? Do we long to return there more than anything in our lives?" I found my dreams in a tree in my backyard. Dorothy found her home in Kansas. Is there a thread of truth running through humanity that always brings us home? I don't know. But I know this: My life was born in the tree that my daddy planted a long time ago. The sounds of my music were planted in my own backyard, and though I travel far to sing and perform, I still feel like I am right at home. I think the people that pay to hear my music are just trying to hear the sounds of their childhood one more time. I know I am trying to hear mine.

My first son was born a couple of years ago. I sing him to sleep at night with that same old guitar made from the tree. He has grown up so fast, and the years are blowing by quicker than I ever dreamed. Yesterday, we walked outside to the backyard and I held his little feet in my hands as I lifted him up to reach the branch of the tree in our backyard. I wondered then, "Is my son reaching for the tree or is he beginning the first step of the rest of his life?"

PRETEND THAT LIFE IS NOTHING BUT A TREE
AND IT'S GROWING CONSTANTLY.
YOUR ONLY RESPONSIBILITY IS TO STAND STRONG
AND GROW IN PEACE.

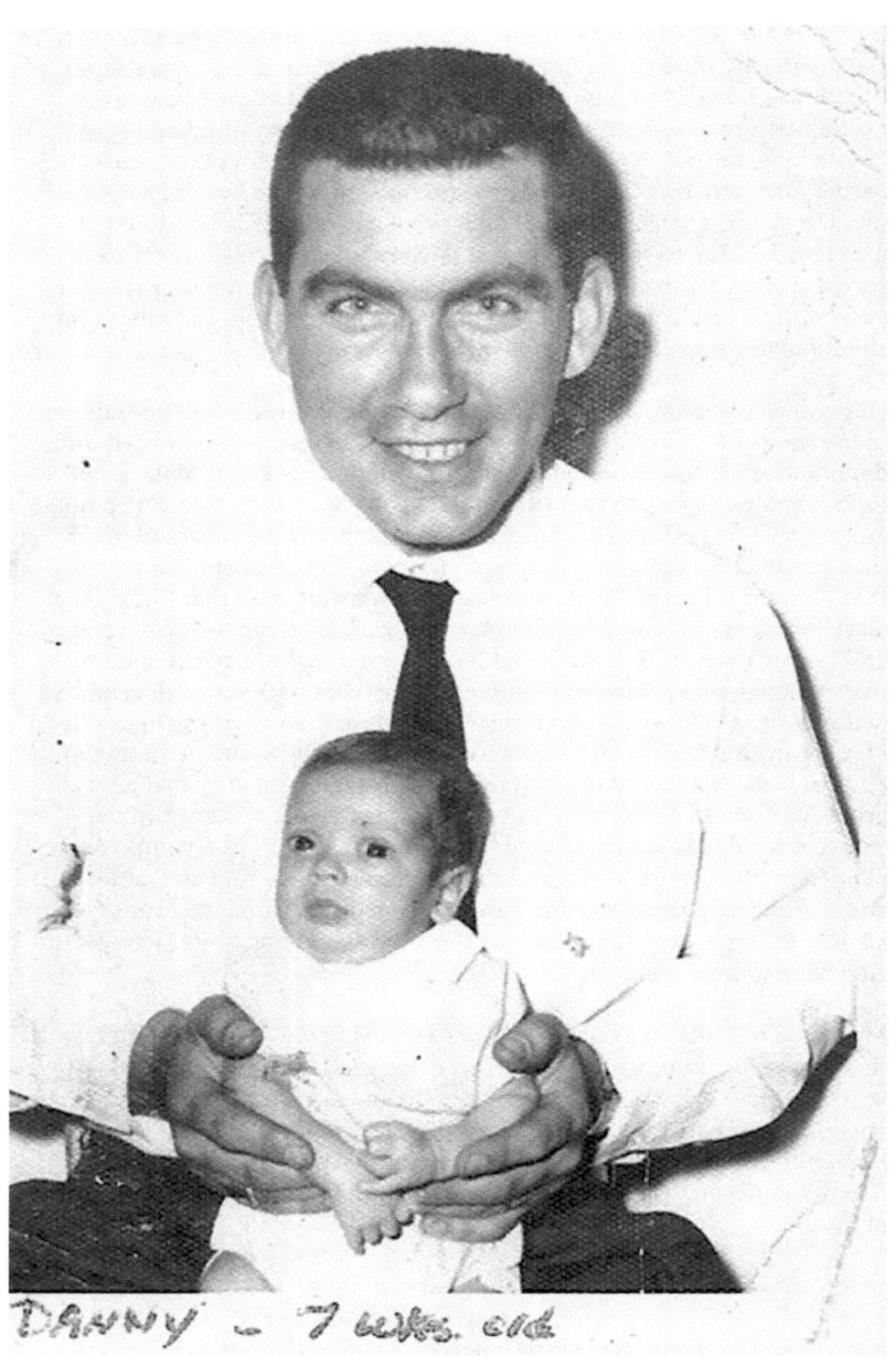

DANNY — 7 wks. old

My first picture. My Dad, Billy Nicholson, and me. Byerly Hospital, 1962.

5

GOD IS NOT DIFFERENT THAN DAD

Moreover, we have all had human fathers who disciplined us and we respected them for it. How much more should we submit to the Father of spirits and live!
HEBREWS 12:9, NIV

Jesus taught in parables and He did so for a reason. It was because we as human beings need earthly stories with Heavenly meanings, something to hang our hats on. In many instances, Jesus found a part of life that we understand...a part of life that we have held and experienced. From the story of the prodigal son to the parable of the seeds, Jesus' stories could get under our skin and win our hearts by catching our resistant and self satisfied minds off guard. A parable is a great work of artistry that Jesus used to protect and project God's wisdom in words.

In much the same way, I began to find parables between the nature of God and the role of a father. As a dad, I began to experience many lasting truths through practical experiences with my sons. What follows in this piece are parables that will hopefully lead you to a greater understanding of God as a Father.

It is indeed hard for us to imagine God as our Father. How can the Creator of the universe actually know the number of hairs on our head? How can He be so close to us? Maybe through these examples of earthly experiences, we can begin to get a glimpse of God as a Father in our lives.

As a child, I remember Sunday evenings at home. We would gather around the television and watch the Sunday night classics. I would lay on the floor with my favorite pillow and enjoy the security of being with my family.

My dad would sit in his old familiar chair. As the night grew later, I would get a desire for my favorite ice cream. During the commercial break, I would make my desire known by announcing how much I would love to have some ice cream to enjoy while watching TV. I would roll my eyes to see my Dad peeking above his newspaper. Invariably, he would always say, "Well Mom, do you need anything from the store?" I knew that was the sign. He would leave the comfort of his chair, gather his car keys and exit out the back door, and I would hear the dull roar of the car engine as he made his way out of the drive. In a matter of minutes, he would return and make his grand entrance. Then with that familiar smile of satisfaction, he would unveil the thing that made his child happy...ice cream.

Down deep inside I remember asking the question, "How can he love me so much?" I would interrupt his evening, and then he would go out of his way to meet my heart's desire. Now I understand. When I became a dad on June 26, 1989, I realize it's not a burden to give to those you love. It is a privilege. That was the first thing I learned about a father's love through experience.

But ultimately, as human beings, we begin to take Love's sacrifice for granted. We lose touch with what it means for Love to go out of its way to meet our needs. Instead of appreciating this privilege, we begin to expect it as a matter of course. Sacrifice is a choice Love makes because of its very nature. Love can't act any differently because, in essence, that's what Love is all about; and for sure my dad loved me.

The reality of his love became clear to me in the summer of 1990. We were at our beach house, a place that dad had worked hard to secure for us. We spent many happy summers there enjoying the fellowship of family. On this particular trip, dad was sleeping a lot. Our concern turned to fear because we all knew dad had a heart problem. A few years before, we learned that he had a rare disease that was slowly incapacitating his heart. It was inevitable that, for my dad to continue to live, he would need a new heart. He had been on a heart transplant list for over a year and a half. The situation had gone on for so long that we had become used to this urgent state of being and unknowingly put away the fact that dad would not last much longer without a new heart.

We left the beach and went straight to the hospital. The doctors decided to keep him there until he died or they found a new heart. It was a serious situation and we braced ourselves for the worst. It's the kind of moment that you don't like to look at face to face. But we waited scared to death or of death. My mom told me that dad had cried for the first time she could remember. I prayed that night. It was all I could do, for I knew when man's hand ends, that's when God's hand begins.

The next morning, we were awakened by the ringing of the phone. It was like an alarm clock and I answered it frantically. I will never forget what the doctor said. "We are flying your dad to Charlotte, North Carolina. You and your mom need to get there as soon as you can." He said that a nineteen-year-old boy had died in a motorcycle accident in Asheville, N.C., and his heart looked like a perfect match for my dad.

I remember it like yesterday, arriving at the hospital and walking in to see my dad. For the first time, I can honestly say, I did not take my dad's love for granted. There is something about final moments that make one realize what is truly important. As I left the room at 10:00 p.m., the thought crossed my mind, "What if this is the last time I see my dad?" At that moment, I turned around and said, "Dad, I love you." He said he loved me, too.

All night we waited. As the sun began to rise, the nurses told us the doctor would be out to talk with us soon. I've never had more respect for someone in all my life than when the doctor met us outside of the operating room and said that my dad's surgery was successful.

A new heart and a new lease on life. But new life is not without a price, and once again I learned a lesson. Because a nineteen-year-old boy lost his life and gave his heart, my dad lived. Every time I see my dad working with the flowers in the yard, walking with my mom on the beach, or playing with my children, I remember that new life always has a price.

I learned a lot from my dad, but now I am one The picture of a Father becomes more real to me with each passing day. The toughest thing about being a father is being patient and forgiving.

One morning I had the task of getting my sons, Taylor and Bryson, to daycare because my wife had bus duty at her school. I faced the usual challenges of fixing breakfast, dressing them, and finally getting them into the car. I noticed as we got into the car, there was a ball point pen on the floor. Any good father knows that this is a dangerous weapon in the hands of a child, especially when you are dressed in a clean, white, cotton dress shirt. By the time I got around to the other side, Taylor had picked up the pen and was writing innocently on a scrap sheet of paper. It seemed relatively safe, but I kept my distance.

As we pulled up to the daycare and I went to get him out of the car, I felt the pen come down across my shirt. As I carried him in, I looked down and noticed that he had struck me across a visible part of my white shirt. With no time to change, I was resigned to the fact that I would have to bear the mark of his mistake all day. But suddenly a feeling came over me that was a complete surprise. Instead of being mad, I felt a sense of pride. It was as if I wanted everyone to know that this was the mark of my son.

As I circulated at meetings and work that day, people would immediately ask me, "What's the mark on your shirt?" "How did that happen?" I found myself telling everyone, with pride, that my son marked my shirt. My reaction to his mistake became the evidence of my love for him. Somehow my love

for him made me blind to his mistake. Love has a way of doing that, especially between a father and a son.

God is not different than Dad in that respect. He is faithful to give us the desires of our heart, even when He has to sacrifice. We, in turn, take Him for granted more times than we can count. Still, He is there with a new heart and a new life, ready to give us all our heart's desires. And when we lift our pen of deep, dark sin against the pure holiness of his heart, He does not condemn us. He wears it as evidence of His everlasting Love for us.

Thanks Dad. I believe I finally understand.

6

WHAT'S IN A NAME

Hallowed be your name.
LUKE 11:2, NIV

The God-mother of my children is an angel named Barbara Mead, affectionately called by all her many friends, "Binky." Since the first day I met her at Baptist College at Charleston, she has remained the greatest example of giving and serving that I have ever known.

We met at the end of my senior year in college. She actually gave me my first job as an admission counselor upon my graduation in 1984. Even though she was my boss, we had an instant connection. Of course, Binky has an instant connection with everyone from the janitor to the elevator operator. She is constantly sharing a smile and a good word of encouragement. But our connection was in some ways divine and we both knew it. There were times when we would stay for hours after work to talk about God's love, the meaning of our lives and dreams. She would listen to me for hours and then in her own special way, she would give me some golden nugget of advice that would lead me down the right path.

During all these many years, she has listened to and supported my dreams in every way possible. There have been cakes, perfectly written cards, dinners at Magnolia's, food and flowers delivered in Nashville, a piano that is a centerpiece in our home, autographed framed prints of all the Wizard of Oz characters in my office, blessings beyond measure bestowed upon my family and children, James Taylor and Neil Diamond concerts, and the list goes on and on.

Of course, these material objects are only a reflection of her spiritual gifts. It really started late nights after work when she would share some of the challenges of her day. I would listen, and in some cases, walk over to touch the leaves on the tree in her office and say, "God is going to take care of a good heart like yours. Just like He does these leaves, He cares about the small things and He certainly cares about you." It was just a small offering in reflection compared to the incredible advice and support she gave to me; but I guess it was timely, and she appreciated the comfort of knowing that God was in control. Our friendship grew out of these moments.

I was determined to help others see the selfless sacrifices she made. She would never seek credit or recognition, but I wanted others to see the light shining in her heart. So I invited the local T.V. station to campus and surprised her by awarding her the "Big Apple Award" which honored her for all the many acts of kindness and service she had given to others. It was a priceless moment. She deserved it more than anyone I have ever known.

It is impossible to capture all the many sacred moments we have shared such as praying in her father's hospital room with her family, the car wash with MaMa Maggie, the Christmas Scavenger hunt with the boys, roses for her and her mother at the concerts. All of these memories represent some of the most meaningful moments in my life. But none of these compare to the moment in the Byerly Hospital parking lot on September 26, 1992. I was always looking for a way to say thank you for all she has meant to me, my family, and all the thousands of students at CSU. On this night in September, I expressed my gratitude in the deepest way I could ever imagine.

I did it with a name. You see, my son, Bryson, was born on this night, and there in the parking lot I told her that we had named our baby boy, James Bryson "Mead" Nicholson. Her last name would be a symbol of my deepest appreciation and love. Her family heritage and all that it means would be remembered in my son's name. What a moment....we cried and laughed with joy....Bryson Mead.

I tell that story because later I wrote a poem to express the reason why I had bestowed on my son the honor of her family name. It was not just a nice gesture, it had meaning, real meaning, and I wanted to put it down in words so that Bryson and others in the world would know.

WHAT'S IN A NAME

"What's in a Name?" the young boy exclaimed,
As his father sat and pondered,
"It's who you are, it's where you're from,
It means you never have to wander
Away from home to distant lands
To seek a shining star
Or roam alone in desert sands
To find your dream afar.
Your home is there within your name
And Son, one thing is true
That faithfulness and friendship both
Are in this name for you."
"But Dad, how does a name mean so much?"
"It means as much as ties that bind
Of memories and love combined
Of laughter, life, and peaceful joy
Of special moments and baby boys
And one day soon you'll understand
It is the name that makes the man."
"What did I do to get this name?
Was it money, power, fame?"
"Nothing son, names are given
For love cannot be earned
The name was here before you came
And speaks of lessons learned.
It came from leaves that whispered
As the wind moved through the trees
Passed down through generations
A Heritage of Meads.
And soon one day you will finally see
That the only reason for a name
Is to leave a legacy."

With innocence the boy said, "Legacy,
What is this word? I believe it is one I have never heard."
"It means some things will never die
That kindness lasts forever
That love and light will soon shine bright
Within the stormy weather.
It means responsibility,
To live and love a Legacy,
And then one day when you face the end
To pass it on.... so it lives again."

7

JUST BEYOND THE FENCE

He will wipe every tear from their eyes.
There will be no more death or mourning or crying or pain,
for the old order of things has passed away.
REVELATION 21:4, NIV

Just Beyond the Fence...
I often heard their stories... stories that they embraced from the past.
Memories that stood like monuments and symbols of yesterday. On those
quiet evenings when I would work with my hands Just Beyond the Fence.
I heard them relive the times they loved, the times they danced in high
school, the times they held hands as youth and ran against the wind, the
sunsets and beaches, full moons and willows...

Just Beyond the Fence...
I often pondered as I arranged my friends in the soil, how this country boy
and city girl found such common ground to stand upon. What bridges have
they crossed to share such warmth and laughter? There was a special union,
an almost magical connection that echoed through the air as they shared
those warm summer evenings.

Just Beyond the Fence...
I knew him well because he was a gardener, too. As he lingered in his dreams
there in the garden of his backyard, we would share the conversations that
most neighbors do, of weather and the burden of daily routines. But I always
noticed when I mentioned her name, there was a light that appeared as if
someone had shattered the darkness of yesterday with hope for tomorrow.
I could tell that his garden, and everything else in his world was centered
around her. Somehow he made me believe that there was some of what used
to be still alive.

Just Beyond the Fence...
But summer time ended and the fall was quietly ushered in. For a season
there was a seemingly cold and melting silence... unlike the days of summer
when their laughter was never ending.

It was a cold winter morning when I saw the flowers on the door...and then... then I knew the reason for this uncommon silence...

Just Beyond the Fence...
As time passed, the spring season came and brought the sound of singing birds, the budding of trees, the smell of the newborn that I so dearly love. But there was only silence...

Just Beyond the Fence...
I began to nurture my day lilies as the days grew longer, planting and working the soil. I was startled one evening by the view of a solemn silhouette standing still, like a statue in the garden...

Just Beyond the Fence...
It was her, without him staring into space. I felt a nudging in my heart to interrupt her silence even though the tasks of the day awaited me. As we began to talk I could tell she needed someone to listen.

Her words came out like water from a broken bottle, spilling from her lonely aching heart. She told me of the notes he use to leave her. She paused as she said he always used to say goodbye with, "Yes, I do love you."

And then she leaped into her favorite remembrance...the final words of one of their many late night talks. "You see," she said, "I was his third wife, yet the time God had given us in the twilight of our days was the best we had ever known. He asked me once, 'Why did I not find you in the beginning? If only we could have started earlier.' I turned and looked into the eyes of his soul and said, 'Lake, we saved the best for last.'

There was silence for a moment, and then out of the back of my mind I heard the laughter, the stories, the echoes of yesterday. And there in her eyes was the reason for it all. It was love, and love never dies.

Just Beyond the Fence...

8

THE GOSPEL OF THE OPPOSITES

These people come near to me with their mouth and honor me with their lips, but their hearts are far from me. Their worship of me is based on merely human rules they have been taught. Therefore, once more I will astound these people with wonder upon wonder; the wisdom of the wise will perish, the intelligence of the intelligent will vanish.
ISAIAH 29:13-14, NIV

Life is complicated. In most cases things are not what they seem. Early in my life I recognized that my decisions usually needed to be the opposite of what I felt. I learned this little by little as I observed that my beliefs were in direct opposition to my feelings or what I was inclined to do. I suppose this tension began to surface as I contemplated God's words in relation to my feelings and actions. For instance, "The least shall be the greatest, the first shall be last, the empty shall be filled," or "The greatest among you shall be the servant." These words began to settle in my heart and emerge as a North Star in the context of my decision-making. For example, in my physical life success is judged by being number one no matter what the cost. But as I stood at the threshold of this reality over and over again, I realized that God noticeably had a different measuring stick. Could I really be successful by coming in last? What is God trying to say?

Through the years, this battle of ideas in my mind and heart encouraged me to use a term that began to make more and more sense to me. The term is, "Gospel of the Opposites." When I make a decision these days, I usually consider the very opposite of my feelings and natural inclinations...the opposite of me. Usually, if I stay in the gray very long, I begin to see that the decision is not about what is best for me, but indeed what is best for another. In a real sense, this process is the foundation for living a life in the flow of love. Why? Because love by its very definition is not about you. It's about God and others. It is a sacrificial relationship with all of life, a place where you die so that God and His truth can live.

No doubt, this is opposite from my natural fallen state which seeks to promote and protect only what is best for me. This is in contrast to what God expects and demands based on His Word in my life. How else can one interpret His resolve to embrace the cross? Did He feel like dying an unjust death on my behalf, or was it His commitment to living a life in the flow of love....a sacrificial relationship with all of life? If you remember, in the Garden of Gethsemane He revealed his human nature by asking "if this cup could pass," but He also revealed His divine nature by crawling up on a cross and dying for my sins. "Not my will, but Thine be done." It is the same way with us. Will we crawl upon our cross for the sake of others? Will we sacrifice our wants and needs for what is best for others? It is a courageous life that claims to believe this truth and then act upon its beckoning call. It is not for children. It is not a game. It calls upon our greatest devotion and resolve to live a selfless life as a true reflection of what we believe and hold true.

Now, let's take the time to walk these truths out in a real life example. The one I am thinking of is in relation to marriage, the union of two people by way of God's Spirit. In God's Word this is serious business. It is a commitment to God as much as it is to another person. That's why in our public vows we state, "In sickness and in health, for richer or for poorer, til death do us part." It does not say, if I feel like it today or if it meets all my needs. Our commitment is that there is nothing that love can't overcome. We are called to be there if our loved one is dying of cancer. We are called to be there if we are living in the depths of poverty. We are called to live in a sacrificial relationship with all of life until we die.

I guess it comes down to how you define love. Let's face it, over 50% of marriages end in divorce in our society, which, by the way, does not make it right. It has always been lonely at the cross. Commitment is not in style, and it's certainly easy to see that there is a longing for *something* that we don't have. What is that *something* that we don't have? Most of my friends who are getting divorced say, "I am not happy." So, what is happiness? What are we looking for that God's love can't overcome? Is it sex? Is it a perfect person that agrees with everything we think and believe? Is it having a family that is stable and the welfare of our children? Why do so many of us think it is the right thing to do to break our public promise to God for our own happiness?

It comes down to keeping one's promise. It means doing what you say and saying what you do. The union of word and deed is the very definition of integrity. The root word of integrity is *integer* which means "whole" as in a whole number. Integrity is when one's words and deeds are in union. They are whole in a sense that the circle is unbroken. That is the symbolic meaning of the wedding band. We wear it to publicly say that our love is whole...that the circle will never be broken and that love is everlasting. In our wedding vows, Debra and I wrote "that we would always love God more than each other." In fact, I think it was stated that I would rather die than love you more than God. There was a reason for that. Even then I thought that our human love could die, but I knew in my heart that God's love would last forever. I wanted to love someone that would never leave, never die. If we both loved God more than each other, then I knew our love would last. That's not to say that we have not had our share of differences and uncomfortable feelings. We have. It's just to say that there is nothing that love cannot overcome, and that commitment lives in our relationship beyond feelings.

The "Gospel of the Opposites" holds true in every human endeavor. We are called, just like Christ, to live in the flow of love and have a sacrificial relationship with all of life. We are asked everyday, and sometimes every minute, to denounce our desires and wishes for the good of others. It may sound contrary to the real world, but it is the only real love there is on this side of heaven, where all this nonsense will be put to rest. It was C.S. Lewis who wrote the passage that confirms these truths in a profound and meaningful way in the last paragraph of his book entitled Mere Christianity. I close with this quote in underlining the meaning of the "Gospel of the Opposites."

> *"The principle runs through all of life from top to bottom. Give up yourself and you'll find your real self. Lose your life and you'll save it. Submit to death, death of your ambitions and favorite wishes everyday and with your whole body in the end: submit with every fibre of your being and you will find eternal life. Keep nothing back. Nothing in you that has not died will ever be raised from the dead. Look for yourself and you will find in the long run only hatred, loneliness, despair, rage, and ruin. But look for Christ and you will find Him, and with Him everything else thrown in."*

9

ONE IN THE SAME:
A GUITAR AND A PAINT BRUSH

Truly I tell you, whatever you did not do for one of
the least of these, you did not do for me
MATTHEW 25:45, NIV

Legacy Road was a dream that came true. It was a vision in my heart and mind to bring together a lifetime of experiences with faith, family, friends, missions, and music to make a memory that would last forever. That's what legacy is all about, a lasting memory that keeps feeding the heart and soul with inspiration toward a common goal.

The plan was to ask all my friends and family, who are songwriters, to offer an original song to be recorded on an album entitled, "Legacy Road." After finishing the recording, we would orchestrate a concert weekend back home in Hartsville, S.C., and raise money for the "Nicaragua Project." It was an attempt to answer such questions as, "What are our talents made for?", "What is the most important thing Jesus wants us to do with our lives?" "How can we use what God has given to us to make a difference?" "Legacy Road" was my answer to these questions.

We finished the album and raised $20,000 during that special weekend in which my sons, Heart of Love band members, Gene Cotton, Michael Johnson, Shannon Tanner, and a couple hundred of our friends enjoyed a time of fellowship and music together. It was a memory that will never be forgotten and if we would have stopped there, it would have been enough. But that's when the real work began. We took the money and decided how it could be best used to minister to the poor. That's what Jesus called us to do. He did not call us to just anyone. He called us to those who needed it the most. In a real sense, we traded in our talent, friendships, and gifts for impact, meaning, and legacy.

Building a legacy in our lives is like taking a trip. In fact, you can make a decision to build your own legacy in the same way. First, decide where you want to go. Then, pack your bags accordingly. Make sure you take all the things you will need for the trip. Depending on where you are going, pack the right clothes, food, a map, and don't forget your guitar. A camera is essential to record your travels because in most cases, the pictures and video will preserve the memories you create. See all the sights you have planned ahead to experience and then when you get back home, show the pictures to all the people you love. Don't forget to tell the stories of your travels because these are the stories that are passed down and kept in our hearts.

What follows is a snapshot of my journal entries from our trip to Nicaragua. Actually, it is a story of legacy, and all the many holy moments we shared and experienced. When you are reading about these moments, think deeply about your legacy. What trip do you want to take in life? What do you want to be remembered for? What will you use your gifts and talents to accomplish? What is your legacy?

LEGACY ROAD: **JOURNAL ENTRIES**

I am sitting in Managua, Nicaragua and wanted to share the experience we had during Christmas holidays, 2009. The writing and recording of the *Legacy Road* album began last year but the real music was finished when we painted a school, installed a cyber cafe with 10 donated computers, and put a brand new roof on Roger and Sonia Gonzalez's home. It was a time to remember, a time of Legacy.

December 27, 2009
We started on December 27 with 20 individuals: Rags Coxe and his son, Rags Jr., Gene and Marnie Cotton and their grandson, Marcus, The Edwards Family, Jimmy and Pam Sanders, Elaine Murray, Tee Gildemeister, Denny Griswold, Jennifer and Sophia Schafer, Ingrid Shoaf, Bryson and me. The first day we got to know each other and cleared out the vines, weeds, and trees which had grown up around the school. It was 95 degrees in Nicaragua and hot was not the word for it, but we didn't seem to notice much because of the excitement of the project.

Before we started, Gene Cotton asked us to join hands in a circle and pray. Instead of closing our eyes, he asked us to keep our eyes open and to look at the school and surroundings. His point was that all our lives we are asked to close our eyes. Many have not opened their eyes to see, and we need to pray with more awareness of our surroundings. We started by saying a prayer with our eyes wide open. That evening we had our first meal in the home where we were staying. Bryson and I had our
44

own room with a bath. The only things in the room were two beds and a computer screen where our host had run a wire that had one TV station that came in at night, fuzzy at best. But it was the family's way of giving us the best they had, and we were touched by their generosity. We took a shower at 5 p.m. The shower was cold water that barely came out of the shower head. The reason we took the shower at 5 p.m. is because all water is cut off from 6 p.m. until 11 p.m. to conserve water. Water is a blessing that we take for granted, but I know that Bryson and I will never take it for granted again. The meal was grilled chicken that was prepared on an open fire in their home.

We sat around tables like the old days. Families in Nicaragua are much closer than ours. They don't have so many distractions, and the only real entertainment is conversation with each other.

After dinner we all went to Roger and Sonia's home and sat outside on the porch and played music and shared stories. Gene and Marnie Cotton sang some songs, and we talked about our work at the school. Interestingly enough, many past friends from the Managua neighborhood dropped by to visit. Gene has been going to Nicaragua since 1990 and has adopted the entire neighborhood. Many friends have been made through the years, and it was a blessing for all that made the trip to have instant friends.

December 28, 2009
The second day, we began to wash down the walls of the school and put the first coat of primer on the walls.

As we worked, the people of the village were inquiring about who we were. They wondered if we were the government spending their money. The government is not trusted in Nicaragua and if you read the history you will learn why. While we worked, so many children came and begged us for money. It breaks your heart when children are hungry and thirsty. This reality is much different than America. For the most part, we do not really know what poverty is to the extent found in Nicaragua. Nothing breaks my heart more than not being able to help a child.

These helpless moments reminded me of an experience Gene Cotton and I had during a previous visit a few years earlier.

We were sitting in a restaurant where a window was open to the street. As we ate our dinner, we observed a young boy sitting by the road. He looked at us with big eyes that seemed to say, "I am hungry." We motioned for him to come inside and we watched him eat what was left on our plates. Gene and I shed a tear during that moment but there was also a joy that filled our hearts. We took a picture of the young man, and to this day, it reminds me of how blessed we truly are. Somehow I knew in my heart that these children are the ones Jesus would have taken care of. It was a powerful moment in my life.

The truth is, it's hard not to respond to every single child. It breaks one's heart to know that children go to bed hungry every night. At the end of the day, we had the primer finished and we were ready to put the colors on the next day. Our evening consisted of the same routine as the previous, and we began to feel like family with our Nicaraguan friends and each other. One blessing during our work was the many conversations we had with each other about our lives and families at home. There was a lot of sharing and seeking to understand why each of us had chosen to be here and help in this way.

I was touched by those I shared with and felt a real bond of God's love. Bryson and I spent the rest of the evening learning Spanish. He taught me for a couple of hours that night, and I actually learned to count to 10 in Spanish. I was proud of his ability to speak Spanish and get me through our days.

December 29, 2009
I started the third day by going to the market with a couple of friends to buy a few items to give back to family and friends who had made our trip possible. The rest of the group began putting the color on the school. When I returned, we worked the rest of the day to insure that we had the biggest part of the school painted.

One might ask, "Why paint a school when there are so many other needs?"

Well, the painting of the school made it possible for everyone in the community to see an outward expression of how important education is and gave them something to feel proud of in their community. It is a constant reminder that the future can be brighter and that the children of Managua have an opportunity through education to have a better life.

46

At the end of the time, we had a brand new school, new friends, and a renewed sense that God has blessed us to help those who are not as fortunate as we are. The whole experience left us humbled by a true glimpse of how much of the world lives everyday. It made us thankful for food, hot water, availability of medicine and healthcare, and simple infrastructure like roads and schools. Most of all it accomplished what I had in mind. It pulled a bunch of musicians together to leave a legacy for their family and friends.

The walls of that school have music painted on them. A guitar and a paint brush became one in the same and in God's eyes they really are. *Legacy Road* is about living past one's life and being remembered for what you truly love and value. I have a feeling when I leave this earth, Bryson and Taylor will find their way down legacy road to Nicaragua and continue to do something for this neighborhood of gracious and beautiful people. That's what's so important about *Legacy Road*. The dream never ends. It counts for something in a real and meaningful way.

Pictured are a few of the Nicaraguan children we met during our mission trip in 2009. The little girl below is Lila Ruth. Today, she has her own family and is a practicing dentist in Nicaragua.

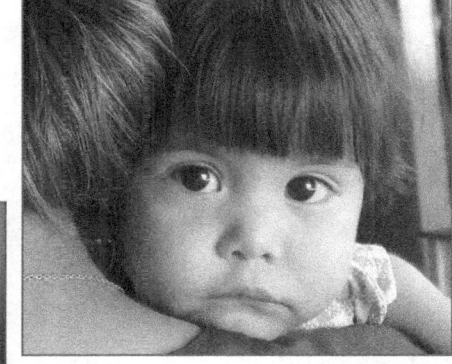

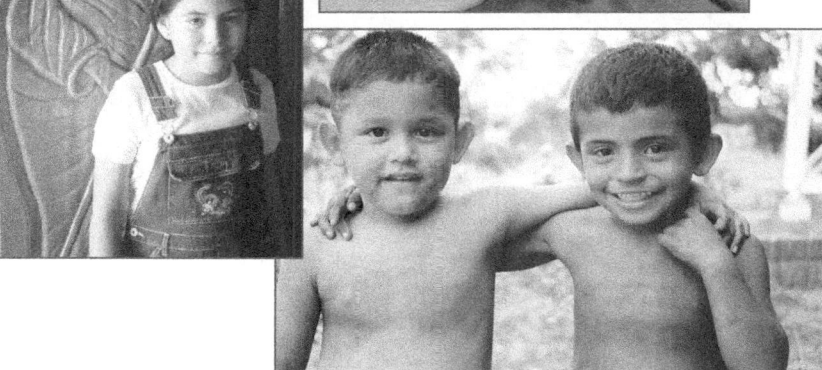

BOSTON MARATHON®
April 17, 2000
MARATHONFOTO

First Boston Marathon, 2009.

IO

THE HEART OF BOSTON

Therefore, since we are surrounded by such a great cloud of witnesses,
let us throw off everything that hinders and the sin that so easily entangles,
and let us run with perseverance the race marked out for us.
HEBREWS 12:1, NIV

Every dream begins at 6:00 a.m. or at least it does in my world.

As I pulled myself out of bed, I checked the weather, fumbled around in the dark for my running shoes, and drank some water. It was still dark outside and I was greeted by the freezing cold as I stepped out the door and started slowly jogging, still half asleep. These were the first steps towards a dream I had considered for a long time...my first steps towards running the Boston Marathon.

Dreams don't happen all at once.

They begin with a vision, a spark of inspiration that leads to seeing yourself living in a preferred future. In this case, I had run five or six marathons and was ready for something out of the ordinary, something that I didn't know if I could do. Well, the Boston Marathon qualified, and I must admit, I was a bit timid as I reviewed what it would take for me to actually accomplish this dream.

Boston is not your regular marathon race. You have to qualify to get an invitation, and the qualifying time I needed was a challenge to say the least. I would have to train for six months and run under three hours (seven minute mile) before I even signed up for the "big race." Then I would have to train another six months before I ran Boston, that is if I qualified in the first place. So I began my journey with this first step on a cold winter morning.

From the start, one is always asking this question, "Why? Why would a person want to go through this grueling routine to run 26 miles and take one's body to the ultimate limit?" My answer was that I wanted to live physically, mentally, and spiritually at my highest level. I wanted to reach my highest potential. I wanted to live and have no regrets. Training and discipline are always behind the glory of a dream.

Suffice it to say, I ran three to eight miles a day during the week. The weekend was dedicated to the long run which started at eight miles and went to 22 miles by the end of the training period. The weekdays were a mixture of slow runs, interval training, and steady pace runs. I finished my training and headed to my qualifying race in Myrtle Beach, South Carolina.

The evening before the qualifying race, I read that my hero and four-time Boston Marathon winner, Bill Rodgers, was going to make a special appearance. I was thrilled. How perfect that I would get to meet someone that I had read about, admired and respected for years. I found my "Runners World" magazine with him on the front cover from 1984 and I thought it would be inspiring to get him to autograph it. I met him that night and told him of my goal to qualify for Boston. He kindly signed the front cover, "Good Luck on your dream to go to Boston."

The next morning was perfect. I ran 2:58 to qualify. I was so excited and began my plan to go to Boston.

After training for another six months, I stepped off the plane in Boston. As I walked through the airport, there were displays of Boston Marathon history and artifacts. There, behind a glass window case, was a pair of Bill Rodger's running shoes from one of his Boston wins. I was inspired and felt my heart rate speed up with every experience. I was living my dream.

The magic and pageantry of this century old race is full of traditions. Over 20,000 runners enjoy the city, tell stories, and share the tension of the upcoming battle. In the midst of this magic, I saw where Bill Rodgers was signing books at the conference center. I made my way to the end of the two-hour line and waited my turn. When I handed him a picture to autograph, I told him the brief story of his good luck wishes in South Carolina and that I made it to Boston!! He signed the picture, "You made it to Boston with will power...Congratulations." (This picture still hangs on my wall today.) It has my running shirt and shoestrings from the race, all framed as a gift from my friends. It is a treasured gift in my life.

I finished the Boston Marathon. It was a satisfying moment in my life. But I wrote all this about the training, meeting my hero, and the race to tell you why I really went to Boston. The real story starts here.

Before the race, it was misting snow and rain so I kept on my warm up clothes until the last minute. Rule number one: Do not start a marathon in wet clothes in freezing weather. You will never warm up during the race and you may risk your health in the process. After realizing it was not going to stop raining, I was perplexed about how to get my clothes and car keys to the pick-up station without getting them wet. A lady in the organizing tent asked me if I would like her to drop my bag at the proper place so it wouldn't get wet. I was very appreciative and thanked her.

After 26 miles in the cold, rainy weather, I was tired and happy but eager to go to the hotel. I stood in line at one of the hundreds of yellow school buses that lined the streets of Boston, each one had large letters identifying the last names of the runners. I saw 'N' and waited my turn to retrieve my clothes and car keys. I told the lady my name, but when she came back to the window, she said, "I cannot find your bag. But I will look again." She returned again and said, "It is not in here." I was stunned. Let me put this in perspective. I was alone in Boston. I had just run 26 miles and now I couldn't find my car keys and clothes.

I decided at this juncture to go back to the starting line which was 26 miles away in Hopkinton. Maybe, I thought, the lady who took my bag left it in the tent and all I have do is pick it up, get in my car, and go back to the hotel. It seemed like the only possible solution at the moment. So I found a bus and sat down in the front seat.

Laying beside the bus driver was a book I once read. It was obvious that she was a person of faith so I asked, "Did you enjoy the book?"

She lit up and said, "Yes, it is one of the best I have ever read." We discussed the meaning of the book over the loud engine of the bus and became quick friends on the hour ride back to the starting line. I told her my story and she was sympathetic to my situation. When we arrived at the place where the tents were set up earlier, they were gone. Nothing. I was lost and all alone in Boston.

The bus driver said, "I can't just leave you here. I'll take you back to Boston and maybe you can find your keys at the lost and found."

I agreed, and she called her boss to ask if she could redirect her route. We talked more on our return to the finish line. When she pulled up she said, "I will wait here for you for an hour but then I will have to leave. Please hurry and good luck."

I ran three or four more miles around the city. At this point, I had run close to 30 miles and was still wet and cold. I asked everyone I could find about my bag: Race directors, lost and found, etc. There was no sign of my clothes or keys.

I went back to the bus driver and said, "I can't find them anywhere. You are

my last hope. Can you help me?" She said, "I have to turn in my bus, but I will give you a ride in my car wherever you need to go."

We turned in her bus and got in her car. I asked her to carry me back to the airport and I would see if the car rental place would give me a key to the car. As she dropped me off, she wished me God's blessings. What an angel she was just to get me to this point.

I went in the rental car office and told them my story. The person in charge said that there were no extra keys and that because the keys were computer programmed, it would be a couple of days before they could get one. It looked like my last hope was a dead end road. I asked, "Is there any other way to get me home?"

"One last shot," she said. "I can call a tow truck and get him to pull a new car back to Hopkinton and bring your old car back here."

I guess she saw the hopeless look on my face and wanted to help this poor human being from South Carolina who was wet, cold, and tired. I plopped down in the waiting area and watched for the tow truck.

When I saw it coming, I was ecstatic. My hope was renewed again. But when the door flung open on the truck, a big, burly man came walking toward the door. As he entered the office, I said to myself, *I'm not getting in that truck with him!* He looked like he had come straight off the street and maybe even from jail. He grumbled something to the office manager, and she pointed to me. He motioned for me to follow him, and we headed outside to the truck. I had no other options at this point, so I reluctantly got in the tow truck after pushing old coffee cups, newspapers, and a half-eaten doughnut out of my seat.

He slammed his truck door and I had still not heard him say a word. He grumbled as he put his keys in the ignition and off we went for another 45 minute ride back to where I had started early that morning. By now, my legs were cramping up, and I was still wet and cold from the race. Now I was getting in a truck with a big, burly Bostonian that I had never even seen before. Honestly, I was scared.

Being friendly, I offered a few comments. He just stared straight ahead, not the least bit interested in talking to me. The silence was deafening, but I surrendered to it and sat as close to the door as I could. Finally, I couldn't stand the silence anymore. "Do you have any kids?" I asked.

He turned to me like I had struck a familiar chord and said, "Yes, I have two."

As we talked, I could tell they were his whole life. We had found common ground and I believe I started to see that this big, grumbling man had a heart. Then we talked about all the challenges he had faced with his kids and he opened up even more. The conversation had become a natural exchange, and if I didn't know any better, I would have thought he was starting to like me a little bit.

That's when he said, "You want to see my picture of Richard, Jr.?"

I searched my mind but I could not remember him talking about Richard, Jr. I said, "You have three children instead of two?"

"Yes," he replied.

I asked him, "Why didn't you mention him before?"

"It's hard for me to talk about him. You know he was named after me. He was my namesake. My name is Richard."

I responded with pride to mimic his feelings and then asked, "Do you want to tell me about Richard, Jr.?"

He turned his head towards me for a moment and I could see the change in his eyes. He told me the story of Richard, Jr. and how he was diagnosed with Multiple Sclerosis when he was young. He talked about how he quit his job to take care of his son; that he figured life and work were not as important as his son, and that he had given 14 years of his life to be with him instead of placing him in a home. "That's not right," he said. "Parents should do that themselves. That's what I did. I stayed home and took care of him, and my wife made the living." From a deep place in his heart I heard him say, "Those were the best days of my life. Do you want to see a picture of him?"

"Yes," I said enthusiastically. He reached into his brown tethered wallet to find a well worn picture with tattered edges. He handed me the picture, and there was Richard Jr. in a wheel chair with his golden retriever by his side. "What a handsome guy with a big smile," I said softly.

"Yep, and a big heart, just like his old man." He immediately was lost in a memory. I could tell it was almost like he was reliving it. "Richard, Jr. loved wrestling."

"He did?" I followed along.

"Yes, one time we heard that all the wrestlers were going to be at the Mall.

So I took Richard, Jr. and guess who got all their autographs and was the life of the party?" "Richard, Jr.," I said with a smile.

"My son loved that day. It was one of the best we ever shared."

I could feel a bit of a glow in the truck. After 45 minutes, two strangers had become best friends and it was all because of Richard, Jr. It was dark now and still raining when we pulled up in the empty parking lot where my car sat all alone. We got out, and he took my car off the truck and began to attach the other car to pull back. As he finished, he looked my way and then walked over towards me. It was still pouring down rain. There was a silence and I felt a lump in my throat, the way you feel when you are getting ready to leave summer camp after a wonderful experience. I struggled to find the words, but then I said, "Richard, I may never see you again, but I want you to know something. I thought I came to Boston to run the marathon, but I didn't. I came here to meet you. You told me one of the greatest stories of love I have ever heard. You gave your life for your son. You sacrificed many years to take care of his needs and do what is right. You are my hero, and I will never forget this moment."

As we stood there in the rain, I saw something release in his face, almost as if no one had ever told him what kind of man he truly was. I watched that big, burly man begin to cry and then extend his arms. There we were, standing in the rain hugging each other in the parking lot. For a moment, I felt as if I had known him all my life.

He stepped back and said, "Thank you."

I will never forget the way he said it.

I got in my car. As I looked out the window, I saw him standing there in the pouring rain. As I drove away, I could see him in my rear view mirror waving goodbye. He stood there until I could no longer see him. It was almost as if he wished I would come back and stay a little longer.

I went to Boston to run the marathon, but I left Boston with an experience that was much greater than dreams, finish lines, and gold medals. I left with a renewed understanding of real sacrifice and love. Every time I look at my Boston Marathon medal hanging in my closet, I remember the heart of Boston.

James B. Edwards and Nicholson.
Mount Pleasant, South Carolina, 2002.

II

INSIDE JOB

Therefore, we do not lose heart. Though outwardly we are wasting away,
yet inwardly we are being renewed day by day. For our light and momentary
troubles are achieving for us an eternal glory that far outweighs them all.
So we fix our eyes not on what is seen, but on what is unseen,
since what is seen is temporary, but what is unseen is eternal.
2 CORINTHIANS 4:16-18, NIV

I attended the Harvard Institute in the summer of 2007. It was intimidating to say the least. I was a small town guy from South Carolina walking by the classroom that Ralph Waldo Emerson studied in. *"What am I doing here?"*

But the moment I went to our first lecture and opened up our textbook on leadership by Bolman and Deal, I felt at home. Why? Well, there on the first page was a line that struck my heart. It stated, *"Ego and self-love block the leader's capacity for empathy."* In the following days, every case study and discussion seemed to lead back to this one theme.

It was a simple, but profound moment in my life. I came all the way to Harvard–the greatest intellectual center in the world– to learn what I had been taught in Sunday School all my life. Pride prevents a leader from empathizing with another human being, from truly putting himself second and feeling what others feel. The goal for a leader is to get inside, not to compromise, but to get inside of another person and reach the goal while meeting the need. It sounds like a contradiction, but remember we are living in a world that considers pushing a fair sport in the field of motivation. Far from the truth, pushing will accomplish the goal, but only for the moment. The truth is we are searching for something that will last.

What will last? What will meet the goal of the organization and the human need at the same time? Sounds like a simple question, but it's not. I think creating a culture that celebrates a pull is more appropriate. What is the difference between a push and a pull?

Well for starters, it goes back to whether the motivation comes from the outside or inside. A push is usually exactly what it sounds like: A physically forced, coercive tactic that has bad consequences, a threat that causes a person to be motivated through fear. It causes anxiety, doubt, and most of all a lack of trust in the motives of the leader.

The follower has to ask, "Does the goal mean more to the leader than the person responsible for accomplishing it?" If so, then it is clearly about the ego of the leader. The follower serves at the will of the leader and is only viewed as one who is putting another feather in the leader's cap. These feelings create stories that define a culture of low expectations and distrust. The domino effect is in place and each person in the organization begins to build fences of resentment and a lack of motivation prevails.

In contrast, a pull starts from within. It is not a forced behavior. It is a voluntary action because it is motivated from inside the person. The leader balances meeting the goal of the organization with the needs of the individual follower.

I learned and more fully developed this concept through my work in fundraising for 25 years and my pursuit of a Ph.D. in this subject. I am absolutely sure it's true. The ultimate financial gift lies at the nexus of the donor's passion and the institution's need. One without the other will compromise the entire outcome. Don't get me wrong, the gift may come to fruition, but it will be far from its optimal level.

In the case of the follower, the leader wants the optimal performance. The gift from the follower needs to be a voluntary decision of the will. It needs to be intentionally motivated by the connection of his/her passion, growth and development as a professional and person. The pull is a driving force within the follower to meet the goal and realize one's full potential. When this happens, it is a win/win situation and fosters a culture of high expectations and trust.

Now, let's try to bring this discussion of empathy to a place of greater understanding. Empathy is the ability for one to walk in the shoes of another. The greatest example of leadership is found in Christ. So how did He carry out His mission? How did He motivate his followers? What is the distinction between a push and a pull in God's eyes?

Well, for starters, we are dealing with God, so it is understood that if you believe in God, He has the authority to push or pull. It is His choice. Early on, He made us and set out 10 rules that would govern the productivity of our lives. We went against those rules in the first scene and continued that pattern until He had to draw a line in the sand and say that there are consequences for not following them. This is just as much a part of love as anything. So He sent a flood to wash away the earth and the moment it was over, He placed a rainbow in the sky to remind us that He will never leave us or forsake us again.

I don't pretend to think for God, but it seems there was a shift in His strategy here. I can see Him stepping back and asking, "Is this really what I want to be to my people? Do I want to push them into loving me ? Or do I want to create a way for them to truly see who I am and voluntarily choose to worship Me and realize their greatest potential in Me?" As the leader of the Universe, can I find a way to get inside of them? Can I become one of them and provide for them an example of what God looks like in the flesh? Can I be empathetic to their needs while still helping them see who I really am?"

So, He decided to give us an example in Jesus. He lived the perfect life and then died upon a cross. Sacrifice became the empathetic response of God to our human needs. He did this so that through the rest of time we would see His love for us and be pulled into a relationship with Him through love. Then, as a loving gift, He decided to go one step further. He would truly get inside of us. If we believed and surrendered to this example, we would have the privilege of God Himself living inside of us. The Holy Spirit would find His home in our heart. It is the greatest example of empathy for the ages. God found a way to live inside us through the sacrifice of His son. What a love story. Can anyone read this story and not say that God went way out of His way to reach His goal and to meet our deepest need?

Peter Gomes, Chaplain at Harvard University for many years, wrote this story in one of his books. It is a story about the first time he met Mother Theresa before she delivered the Harvard Commencement Address. He was standing alone backstage with this little saint of a woman and decided that he would try to talk with her before the address. She was standing face forward when he began to talk, "Where have you been Mother Theresa?"

She stared straight ahead and replied, "I do not know." Nothing more and nothing less.

"Well, then, where are you going next?"

"I do not know."

Finally, he decided to ask one final question that might illicit some deeper response, "Doesn't it please you to see all these students gathered around you, trying to touch you, and learn from you?" She finally turned to him and said, "It pleases Jesus."

Later in the speech, she coined one of her greatest quotes. In the midst of the intellectual capitol of the world she said, "We can do no great things; only small things with great love."

That is empathy at its very best. That is what God did for us and indeed that is how we should relate to others as we work, love, and find our being in this world. It is an inside job and it always will be.

Senior year, Hartsville Red Foxes basketball team, 1980.

12

THE CHAMPIONSHIP RING

Am I now trying to win the approval of human beings, or God?
Or am I trying to please people? If I were still trying to please people,
I would not be a servant of Christ.
GALATIANS 1:10, NIV

I wore floppy socks when I played basketball as a kid. Day after day, I dribbled a ball like there was no tomorrow. Between my legs, behind my back, over and over again I practiced to be the best ball handler I could be. It was a way of life and Pistol Pete was my idol. In fact, when my two boys were old enough to hold a basketball, I made them watch Pete Maravich videos like they were in church. I have home videos where they are dribbling down the street between their legs, doing all the drills. It was as much a part of their upbringing as anything.

Pistol Pete Maravich was an innovator, a dreamer way ahead of his time. He did things with a basketball that others only dreamed about. I wanted to be just like him. A lot of kids wore floppy socks, and I was determined to play the game with the same magic that he did. He was magic, and he inspired a multitude of young ball players just like me.

That's why I was so excited when I heard my mom and dad say that we were going to see Pistol Pete play in Charlotte, North Carolina. I could not believe it and I counted the days down until the time arrived. Pistol was playing for the New Orleans Jazz and they were scheduled to play against the Denver Nuggets on October 4, 1975. I was like a kid at Christmas. The level of anticipation was at a very high level and it took my breath away when I saw him run on the floor. There he was, floppy socks and all. He scored 33 points that evening, and I remember a couple of behind the back passes to go along withthe shooting exhibition. It was a night to remember.

After the game, I asked my mom and dad if I could please try to get his autograph. They let me make my way down to the court. I saw him and ran to ask him to sign my program. Around the bustling crowd, I raised my program in the air, and he signed some scribbling that I could not read. I knew my friends could not read it either so I stuck it up in the air again, and he scribbled on it for a second time. I was so disappointed and I know the security guard standing near me saw the frustration on my face. He looked at me and said, "Hey kid, you see that door right there?"

"Yes sir," I replied.

"If you go out that door and run around the circumference of the building, you might catch Pistol Pete coming out the dressing room door."

I ran out the door like gangbusters and sprinted with all my might around the coliseum. When I finally made it around, I looked up and saw a lone figure coming out the door. It was Pistol Pete Maravich and there was no one between me, him and the bus. Out of breath, I walked up to him and said, "Pistol, would you sign my program again? I could not read what you signed inside."

He looked at me with a sparkle in his eyes and said, "Here kid, hold my bag."

I stood there and held the bag where the sacred floppy socks resided while he signed my program with perfect precision. "Pistol Pete" was inscribed on the program right above the NBA legend Hall of Fame player Elgin Baylor. As he made his way to the bus, I walked away with the biggest grin of satisfaction a 13-year-old kid could possibly have. It was a moment in my life that I will never forget.

Later in life, Pistol Pete died of a heart attack while playing a pick up game of basketball, but not before he had made it public that he had become a Christian. I heard his testimony on a cassette tape that a friend shared with me. He said words on that tape that inspired me more than his playing ever did. He said, "I would rather have Christ in my life than all the championship rings in the world." I knew a championship ring was the one thing he never accomplished, and to place Christ above his whole life's ambition was very meaningful to me. It touched my heart in a deep and profound way. I still watch Pistol Pete on video and to this day I am inspired by has incredible talent and magic. But it was his profession of faith in Christ that made all the difference in my life. Here is a man that had everything I ever wanted and all he desired was Christ. That was the winning moment...the icing on the cake...the biggest testimony of my life.

Thanks, Pistol. Somehow I know you are playing basketball in heaven with the angels, and as far as the championship, you won the ring and gave it to me.

Dive at the Line Club. Captured right before my dive that won an 800 meter race for Baptist College. I was scraped up for weeks, but elated to have run a 1:53.3 for the win!

13

LITTLE THINGS MAKE A BIG DIFFERENCE

He replied, "Because you have so little faith. I tell you the truth,
if you have faith as small as a mustard seed, you can say to this mountain,
'Move from here to there' and it will move. Nothing will be impossible for you."
MATTHEW 17:20, NIV

In the summers, I use to spend time reading books on my back porch. One of the books I found that intrigued me was on Jim Ryun, the great American miler. It fascinated me because he was a young boy who grew up in Kansas without a lot going for him. In fact, he was labeled an "ugly duckling" of sorts and then he propelled to stardom as the first high school runner to break the four-minute mile. I loved it...a nobody who found the pot of gold.

I loved basketball. During a workout my 11th grade year, I found myself way ahead of my teammates during a two-mile conditioning run. When I finished, my basketball coach looked at me and said, "Guess what you are doing this spring? You're running track." It was a gift that God gave to me and that spring I found that I had a talent for running. I made the top eight in the state championship and I broke the mile record for my high school; one that had been standing for twenty years - 4:28.4. My senior year I followed up with a third place finish in the state with about the same time and I found myself being recruited by colleges for a scholarship. It was a blessing in every way and I loved running.

I remember looking at a Baptist College at Charleston track team brochure. This small private college in Charleston, South Carolina, was a Division I program and was known for its track teams. In fact, Coach Howard Bagwell and Jim Settle had built their entire athletic program around track. So I dreamed about the possibilities. I was called for an interview at the college and I immediately accepted. My parents and I went to Baptist College to sit down with a gentleman named Coach Tad Talley. He had been a distance runner and was now the track and field recruiter for the college.

As we went into his office, I had one thing in mind. No, it was not to get a scholarship. It was to find the kind of place that would nurture my Christian faith. I know that sounds unbelievable, but the truth is, I had a car accident the year that changed my life. I wanted a coach and place that would encouraged my faith, and deep in my heart that is what I was looking for.

We sat down and began to talk when he said he needed to go and get something, so he left the office for a few minutes. During his absence, I got up from my chair and looked on his desk. I remember it as a moment of curiosity. But when I looked on his desk, I saw a small, white business-size card with red letters written on it. It was Psalm 110 - "Let everything that has breath praise the Lord - Praise Ye the Lord." I was struck. When I heard him coming back into the office, I quickly sat down so he would not notice that I had been snooping around his desk. He sat back down and I quickly announced to my mom and dad's surprise, "I am coming to Baptist College at Charleston!"

Coach Talley looked at me and replied, "We have not even talked about the scholarship."

I said, "I know, Coach, but this is where I want to be."

Thank God, he gave me a scholarship, but that was a very important moment in my life. You see I made a decision based on my relationship with God, not running, academics, or anything else. The blessings that first step gave me are immeasurable. I had a great track career, received my degree, met my wife, Debra, started my career in higher education before I graduated; and I began my music ministry. All my friends and passions were based on that one moment and a Bible verse - God's Word.

If that was the end of the story that would be enough but the best is yet to come. I never really shared that with anyone because I was just following my impulses and listening to the voice in my heart. I was working at Charleston Southern University (as it is called today) and coming out of the library basement one day when I looked up and saw Coach Talley coming from the parking lot. I had not seen him in nearly 10 years because shortly after I came to college he left to go to another college. I was delighted and ran to meet him.

"Hey, Coach, how are you?" I said, "Great to see you again," We chatted for a few minutes when I looked at him and asked, "Coach, did I ever tell you why I came to Baptist College?"

He said, "No Danny, you didn't."

I said, "Well, remember the day you left the office during my recruiting visit? I got up and looked on your desk and saw a small white card with a Bible verse on it. I had been praying that I could find a Christian coach to train and learn under and you were that coach."

He paused for a moment and then he moved his glasses down from his eyes. I could tell that something I said had moved him because I swear I saw a tear fall from his eyes. He finally responded, "Danny, keep an eye out for the mail in the next couple of weeks I have something I want to send you." I promised I would and we left the parking lot.

A couple of weeks later, I received a letter in the mail addressed from Coach Tad Talley. When I opened it, there was the small white business card I had seen that day under the glass top on his desk. I turned it over and there written in pen on the back was a message. It said, "To Thad Talley...from Jim Ryun....1972." I found out later that Jim Ryun had worked with Coach Talley when he coached at Kansas University. They had become good friends and Ryun had been a meaningful influence on Coach Talley's Christian commitment. He gave it to me because it had influenced my Christian life. I still have that card today. It reminds me that little things make a big difference. Now, I don't know how God orchestrates all these things but I do know this...all the blessings of my life came out of that little card and the foundation of my life in ministry started in that moment in his office.

Don't underestimate the power of some ordinary moment. God will use the smallest of things to carry you where He wants you to go. Little things make a big difference.

November 8, 1973
Danny Nicholson
11 years old

Being a Christian

Being a Christian is
sometimes hard, when
you're with your friends
you have to always be
on guard. Being a Christian
is to take a step forward
and to always be ready
to witness, for the Lord.
And to read the Bible
and pray everyday, to
a Christian it means

A poem I wrote when I was 11 years old.

14

A NIGHT OF SORROWS

I tell you the truth, you will weep and mourn while the world rejoices.
You will grieve, but your grief will turn to joy.
JOHN 16:20, NIV

I was brought up in a Christian home and attended a Christian elementary school until I was in the 6th grade. I remember hearing the Word of God everyday. It was placed in my heart from a very early age. My memory carries me back to moments when I was moved by God's Spirit and felt a deep sense of His presence in my life. The music and message of church and school often moved me deeply. I wrote this poem, "Being a Christian," when I was 12 years of age on November 8, 1973.

Being a Christian is sometimes hard
When you are with your friends you have to always be on guard
Being a Christian is to take a step forward
And always be ready to witness for the Lord
And to read the Bible and pray everyday
To a Christian it means nothing what other people say
We should just keep praying and doing His will
God's plan we should always try to fulfill

I am glad I kept this poem because it reveals to me that I was thinking of my life as a Christian at an early age. I was mindful of God's place in my life and the truth is I was scared of God. I was not scared in a bad way. I just feared and believed that I had a responsibility to live up to His standards.

When I was eight years old, I started playing basketball. The game became my life. I noticed that the better I became, the more people loved me. Soon I recognized that this game enhanced my popularity and I wanted to "fit in" like every young person. So I played night and day. If I heard a basketball bouncing in the neighborhood, I would hurriedly eat my supper and run to the game. Some older boys in my neighborhood started telling me, "You are good for your age" which fueled my desire and motivation. That's when I asked my mom and dad to let me go to public school. I knew that if I was going to get a college scholarship, I would have to play with real players and the talent was noticeably stronger on the other side of the fence.

So my parents enrolled me in Carolina Elementary School during my 6th grade year. I began to excel in basketball and my identity was formed by my success on the court. By my 10th grade year in high school, I was starting guard on the team. In fact, during my first varsity basketball game, I was fouled with 2 seconds left in the game against Lancaster and shot two free throws to win the game by one point. The Coach told me in the huddle before I went out to shoot the free throws that he would give me a Pepsi® if I made them. I still have the Pepsi®can that he gave me.

My dreams were coming true. Little by little, I placed God on a shelf. I was serving me and building my kingdom instead of His. It's easy to do. I took my eyes off what was most important and began to think that the world revolved around me. I am not proud of my decisions but it is part of the journey and now I realize that God allowed me to stray so that I could get closer to Him.

It was a cold, September night after a party in Kelleytown. I was bringing the homecoming queen and her friend home when I experienced "a night of sorrow." I always drove fast because that was cool. On this particular night, I was racing down the highway with my music blaring as loud as it could go. I remember the car beginning to spin around and around until we came to a dead stop. I looked around and the girls in the car with me were sitting still like mannequins. As blood trickled down my face, I reached over and shook the girl sitting next to me. Thankfully, she moved and I helped her out the car. I went and looked at the girl who had just decided to get a ride with me. She was mangled and badly hurt. Her face had hit the tree through the window and she was lying still. My first thought was that she was dead. I shook her a little and saw her move. I remember saying, Thank God." I had not thought of God in years. I picked her up and laid her gently on the ground and said to her, "I am so sorry... I take this back." But it was too late. You can't take back what you have already done. My decisions had brought me to this "night of sorrow."

The ambulance came while I held her hands from her face and stared into her eyes. They took her to the hospital and I remember her screaming with pain, not knowing whether she would live or die. That night as I laid in my hospital room, my whole world turned upside down. I felt like I had nowhere to go. It was all a bad dream that I wanted to take back, but of course I couldn't. As I stared at the ceiling in my room, I felt this overwhelming sense of God's presence.

No, I did not hear a voice. I just felt a comfort, a presence, like an old friend who taps you on the shoulder. I felt like something was about to explode in me if I did not surrender to His call. It's unexplainable, no words can paint the picture. But I knew Who it was, not some religious feeling, but someone real that was calling me home.

I said, " Lord, I have been running from you. But I need you now. I surrender."

From that moment on, I have been resolved to follow God's way. Make no mistake, I have fallen so many times, but that is simply not the point. We all fall down. It's about the direction we go when we get back up. Being a Christian is not playing perfect. There's only One that is perfect and that's why we need His grace and mercy in our lives. With all the ups and downs, my life has been wrapped in God's love and it all started on this "night of sorrow."

God's Word promises in Romans that "All things work to the good for those who are called according to his purpose." My life is evidence of that truth. The Bible is full of people who failed miserably and made bad choices, who made it through their "night of sorrow" and found everlasting peace on the other side.

Peter is the greatest example of one who had everything. Jesus gave him the keys to Heaven and hell, called him the Rock of the church, gave him the power to walk on the water. Yet in his lowest moment, Peter denied Christ. After his "night of sorrow," he was restored and received the power to raise Dorcas from the dead.

King David was a "man after God's own heart." As a young man, he claimed victories in God's power that were honored across the land. Yet in a moment of weakness, he committed adultery and murder. We recognize the wars he faced in his soul when we read the Psalms. It was agonizing and painful, but God restored him through repentance. I am not alone, and you are not either. God is there and knows your heart. A "night of sorrow" can turn into joy in the morning and that's exactly what happened to me.

I remember a few years ago, my friend and I made our way to Hartsville on that same road. As I turned the corner, I said, "Let's stop for a minute and look at my altar." We stopped, and there I stood in front of the tree that was hit that night. The scars on the tree from the accident were still there, and I remembered the sorrow and pain of that September night. I took a picture and said a prayer. I thanked God for the sorrow and pain of that unforgettable moment.

On my desk, I have an Eldorado emblem that was hanging off the car when I went to look at the wrecked vehicle in the junkyard. I pulled it off and have kept it ever since. When I look at this emblem, I don't see sorrow or pain. I see the transformation of my life. I see a symbol of how sorrow becomes joy. I see a lifetime of blessings beyond my wildest dreams. I see God's work in my life.

Conche Cafe. Garden City, South Carolina. 2018.

15

WILL YOU COME TO ME IN MY DREAMS?
Every calling begins with a story...

*And it came about that as he journeyed, he was approaching Damascus,
and suddenly a light from Heaven flashed around him.*
ACTS 9:3, NIV

After thirty years in higher education, I was serving as Vice President for Advancement at Winthrop University in Rock Hill, South Carolina. I was relentlessly pursuing my lifetime dream of becoming a college/university president. But my heart was restless and after going through many trials and tribulations, I had become disenchanted with political bureaucracy and the mired muck of man. I had begun to ask God, "What do you truly want Debra and I to do in this life? Is this really the path that you want us to follow?" I was thrust into the storm of a major leadership change and the uncertainty of the future lingered in the balance. I was at a crossroads and the weight of the world was on my shoulders.

Debra and I endured a year long journey of the heart, soul, and mind. Some days went on forever and I stood eye to eye with the reality of a battle between my ego and my soul. I sat in silence for days, praying, writing, reading, and seeking God's voice. This is where I learned that silence and stillness are the languages of God. I painfully waited for His instruction. It was a standoff with the realities of life and the promises of God. Even though it was unbearable at times, there were moments of clarity when Gods peace and direction interrupted my pain and brought me closer to understanding the meaning of my life and the gift of His peace and presence no matter the circumstance.

This part of my journey unexpectedly came to an end in July 2016.

Here is my story of revelation, redemption, hope, and grace: Debra and I were sitting at our favorite seafood restaurant in Garden City, South Carolina in July of 2016 while waiting for a table. A little African American boy (maybe five or six years old) was running around us (or should I say he ran through us) playing with his toy animals and asking us, "Do you want to play with me?"

His eyes were as big as buttermilk biscuits and his innocent heart and contagious smile stole our hearts. He kept coming back and forth until he finally stopped and asked, "Do you want to sleep over with me tonight?" We laughed and he continued to run around us with reckless enthusiasm. I noticed a white couple who were watching him intently and so I walked over to talk with them.

"That is a fine young man you have there." I said.

The lady said. " We are his foster parents."

Because I am an adopted child, I thanked them for showing him love and giving him a home. We exchanged a few pleasantries and then I went back to sit with Debra and continue to wait for our table.

He continued to run back and forth until they're name was finally called. The little boy asked us if we wanted to go eat with them one more time and then they went up the stairs to find their table. Debra and I looked at each other like something really special was happening but we were not sure except that we had fallen in love with this precious child.

A few minutes later, our table was called and we went in to see them sitting at their table. We spoke with him again and then we went to sit down at our table overlooking the ocean. It felt as if there was something in the air, some magical kind of love that we could not describe. It all seemed like slow motion and we were both trying to understand why this little boy had captured our attention and stolen our hearts.

We began to talk about the many blessings God had given us in our lives and our love for children. We discussed our desire to do something that would thank God for the rest of our lives. Our conversation was alive with hunger and thanksgiving. Little did we know, our answer was resting in that small little African American boy who had stolen our hearts with his wild enthusiasm and innocence.

At that moment, the little boy and his foster family came around the corner to say goodbye. They lingered at our table and stood at the threshold of our time being over. The little boy asked us to come and sleep over one more time and then he jumped in Debra's lap, looked her in the eyes, and said eight words that changed our lives. He said, "Will you come to me in my dreams?"

We were struck in that moment and fully aware that we were standing on holy ground. Everything seemed to stop around us and we felt wrapped in a love that we had never known before. As the little boy walked away, I looked at Debra and said," I dont know what just happened, but our lives will never be the same."

A few months later, I noticed the job announcement for President of Connie Maxwell Children's Home and told Debra, "I think I know what that little boy, a messenger from God, was sent to say to us. God was calling us through him to finish our story. He was calling us to do something bigger than ourselves. God reminded me that He was there when I was born all alone. He was there to make sure a maintenance worker and school teacher picked me up and gave me a home. Now, He wanted me to give other children the precious gift that He had given me.

We are now serving as President and First Lady of Connie Maxwell Children's Home in Greenwood, South Carolina. Our lives have never been so full of peace and purpose. Ruth Graham, Gene Cotton, Jeff Francisco, Kevin Jones, Brooks Shumake, Barbara Mead, Randall O'Brien, and my mom came to our "New Beginnings" celebration and we have been ushered into a new era of ministry and love. Every time we hold these broken, abandoned, and lost children in our arms, we remember God's gift to us and His unfailing love and grace. Our dogs (Summer and Marley) are running in the backyard. The cathedral oak trees are reaching towards heaven. The sound of children playing outside are ringing in our ears. Christmas lights are shining across the campus, welcoming the beginning of celebration for a child that came to rescue us from ourselves. Maybe, just maybe, I was born for this moment and oh what a moment it is!!

Now to sit quietly in this dimly lit room and listen to the voice of God whisper in my soul. "You can stop running around frantically packing your bags, preparing for the journey.

Look up my child!!
Be still....You are home.
Unpack your bags, take a deep breath, and remember.

You are home in "my own backyard."

POEMS

A poet is always trying to capture the moment, carving out the beauty and joy of its meaning, and then make it last forever. Poems are a way of making time stand still and reliving "holy moments" over and over again. Like a picture that is framed or a song that is recorded, poems preserve the "spirit" of a moment and then speak to it like waves in the ocean, pounding on your heart while leaving a salty mist across your face. These poems hold so many beautiful, lasting moments in *my own backyard*.

Taylor and Bryson praying during a photo session for the "Heart of Love" album at Ashcraft Studio, Hartsville, South Carolina. Photo credit, Steve Roos.

16

PRAYER FOR LEGACY

Start children off on the way they should go,
and even when they are old they will not turn from it.
PROVERBS 22:6, NIV

This poem was written for my sons one night as I watched them sleep. It is a prayer that they will both have a legacy as godly men. We need to teach our children about their responsibility of faith and love through the seasons of life. Tomorrow is in their hands, and my prayer is that they will take their role as leaders of faith seriously.

Still as you both sleep

Innocent and young

Unaware of the world around you

I sit and watch you sleep until late in the night

The small flickering light beside your cribs

Toys scattered across the room

As I brush your cheek

A tear gently trickles down my face

It falls on you and I wipe it away.

You are my sons

The only flesh and blood I have ever known

The very heartbeat of my life

I close my eyes and see you both growing up

Every minute I wish to stop and hold

But even now time is moving on

Yes, it seems like yesterday when you were born

But you have already taken your first step and said my name.

God I loved it when you said my name

It made me understand why I live

And soon...all too soon...the years will pass by

I see your first day of school

The games you will learn to play

In and out the back door you both will go

Another day of hide and seek

And make believe pretend and then
I will tuck you in

And watch you sleep again

You will have your glory days

They are just around the corner

Football games and baseball cards

Senior Prom and the day you get married

And then the night that you sit quietly and watch your son sleep

Life is a circle, my sons,

That never ends

And yes, one day you will know how very much I loved you both

My only prayer as I sit and watch you breathe

Is that God will hold you in His Hands

For you see I don't have all the answers

And sometimes I don't know if I have any at all

I have to depend on Love to guide you

Your little brown eyes have not seen the hatred of man

And your silky smooth skin has not felt

The cold wind of a stormy, raging world

Before I prayed tonight I thought of these things

And I searched my mind to think of a way to protect you both

To shelter you from this world I have come to know

To fight and defend you from all the battles you will face

I searched every corner of my mind

But I found no answers

And falling to my knees I prayed this prayer

For you see this is all I have to depend on

When all else is gone
Love remains
Oh God, just as You have touched my life
Reach out now and place your strong but gentle hand on my sons
Teach them Your ways
Let them know that it is not weakness to say I love you and
serve the needs of others
Let them know the peace and abundant life that God has given
Use me, as unworthy as I am,
To show them how to pray
And to read Your words of truth and justice
To stay steadfast in Your loving will
There is nothing more to say
This is my Prayer for Legacy
Sleep now, my sons, for tomorrow will come all too soon
And then I can only hope that you will stay where your father has placed you
In the Hands of God.

Nicholson's mother, **Mary**.

17

HER LOVE LIVES IN ME

Her children arise up, and call her blessed
PROVERBS 31:28, NIV

This poem was written for my mother. There is no way to describe the impact she has had on my life. I remember writing this during my high school years for some special event to try to express all that she means to me. There are no words to adequately thank her for the sacrifice and commitment she poured into my life.

Under her wing of loving care
Secure to seek the world
She softly leads my pathways clear
In arms so gently curled
Curled around my every need and under all my fears
She rocked me in my cradle
She wiped my flowing tears
I've watched her use the patience that I'll never understand
And when I'd fall she'd brush off my knees and I'd go back to play again
She'd peak behind the curtains to watch me cross the street
She'd read me bedtime stories then wrap me in clean sheets
She'd listen to my spelling words and poetry in school
And when I lost my temper she always kept her cool
Messy socks, washing clothes, practice late at night
Gained my respect of love in her that never left my sight
To scratch my back or kiss my cheek was always understood
I guess she never minded cause if she could she would
When I sit and think alone, I see I'm what you are
Cause when I look into my heart I always reach the stars
You are my heart of lasting love

And God knows in the sky above
That in my prayers of everyday
I find myself begin to say
I may not tell her every day of every year
But one thing in my every move is constant and so clear
That I'm thankful for my mother and she lives inside of me
Cause where I go and who I'll be
Her love lives there in me

18

WHITE THINGS ARE ELEGANT

I looked, and there before me was a white horse! It's rider held a bow, and he was given a crown, and he rode out as a conqueror bent on conquest.
REVELATION 6:2, NIV

I wrote this poem during an interim class of poetry in January, 1982, at Charleston Southern University. It's simply a collection of words that speaks to the beauty, power, and elegance of "white things." White things symbolize purity and when collecting these images, God revealed the holy majesty of His creation and righteousness. There is power in purity and simplicity.

WHITE THINGS ARE ELEGANT

Seagulls and lace
Cotton that blooms
Popcorned clouds upon the tree
Old Southern mansions
With columns dressed in pearls
Milky...marbled...
Marsh mellowed moons that spring
From the fields
Dispersed in the wind as a wish
Like unicorns bouncing on the breeze
The opal dancers entertain the waves
As the mountains tip their hats
The snow...
Gently...
Falls...
Like a dove gliding through the thick air

A solitary sand dollar lying on the beach
Bleached by age...painted by time
The sheep grazes
Bubbled bathed in wool
Lathered in innocence
The empty space upon this page...
So quiet...so strong

19

SLEEPING IN MY DREAMS

Blessed are the pure in heart, for they will see God.
MATTHEW 5:8, NIV

While attending the Council for Advancement and Support of Education (CASE) conference I was affected by a inspirational speaker in one of the sessions. After the session ended, I went straight back to my hotel room and wrote this poem. *Sleeping in my Dreams* describes the awakening of one's soul to dreams, returning to a time of innocence when dreaming was commonplace. The line, "I took my wings down from the attic... brushed off the dust," perfectly described my inspired state of being. So many live their lives "sleeping in their dreams." This poem calls us to awaken from our sleep and live out our dreams.

I was walking in my sleep and sleeping in my dreams
Until I awakened one morning
By the touch of a hand on my shoulder
Or maybe it was the words that touched my soul
As the sun slowly danced into view just beyond the horizon
It felt as if someone was in the room
A friend who tapped me on the shoulder
Someone breathing behind me
But when I turned around...there was no one there...only the silent presence of
some forgotten day in my youth
Yet I still felt the staring eyes...the warm touch
The words stirred the stillness of my sleep
And awakened me to the time when I was a child
To taste the innocence once again
The fresh snow of a forgotten dream
The flower slowly budding in the spring

The smoldering sun of a hot summer day
I opened my eyes and saw that the world was much smaller than I had imagined
I felt as though it transported me back to lay on the grassy
knoll with my hands behind my head
Connecting the stars in the sky
The fresh smell of cut grass on the baseball field
The moment I believed I was an astronaut or a fireman
Oh, the sweet innocence of my childhood
When dreams were as thick as fog hovering above the field.
All of a sudden I could see again
The possibilities endless...the clouds within my reach
I took my wings down from the attic
Brushed off the dust
And flew to the highest place I could find.
The sweet taste of dreams made me drunk with belief
I staggered across the Field of Dreams
To touch what I had long forgotten
And there...I was fully alive.
My heart beat fast...dizzy with delight...a tear rolled softly
down my cheek
And fell upon the garden of my heart.
The dry land nourished and the seeds that lie still and
stagnant
Burst into Beauty
Then I heard a voice say, "The gift cannot be compromised."
Raise it up upon the mountain
Show the world your love
Speak Love...Sing Love...Live Love.
I was walking in my sleep and Sleeping in my Dreams
Until I was awakened one morning.

Bryson, Danny, and Taylor Nicholson, 1996.

20

PLAYGROUND NOISE

Children are a heritage from the Lord, offspring a reward from Him.
PSALM 127:3, NIV

This is another poem I wrote during the interim semester of college in January 1982. It is a picture of a children's playground and all the different noises that are connected to children playing. It also speaks to the disappointment at the end of recess. Oh how I loved to play and dreaded when the bell would ring to call us back to class. The sound of a playground is magical. I can still sit and watch children play and wish I were one of them.

Tick...Tock...Tick...Tock...The little children listen to the sound of the clock
As their candy coated dreams seem to melt in their minds
And the sweetness of the playground is the treasure they will find.
Ring... Ring...goes the long awaited bell
As they burst out the door where their fantasies expel
To the castles in the sand and the jungle on the rail
Whee!! Whee!! Push me, please
'Cause I'm swaying in the sky and the clouds are on my knees
Skip Skip Skip Skip Skip Skip Skip
I'm jumping the rope as fast as a whip
And the Bomp Bomp bouncing ball of the boys
Is the background beat of the playground noise
Hippety... Hippety Skip... jump... plop
As the sound of the Hop Scotch game won't stop
And the little girls snicker Hee... Hee... Hee
As they just got caught by the old oak tree
Yet the recess ends with the sound of the bell
And the silence sits so still...
And the sound of the wind and the lonely toys
Was the only sound of the playground noise

21

THE SOUND I NEVER HEARD

Shout for joy to the LORD,
all the earth, burst into jubilant song with music;
make music to the Lord with the harp,
with the harp and the sound of singing
Psalm 98:4-5, NIV

This poem was written about Jim Croce during my college days. Jim Croce was one of my heroes because he wrote with such poetic brilliance. I remember listening to his music on a blue eight track tape cartridge on the side porch of my house when I was eight years old. It was the first tape that I bought and I loved listening to songs like "I've Got a Name," "Alabama Rain," and "I Have to Say I Love You in a Song.' These songs were later the foundation for my songwriting, and I still love to listen to them today. This is how I felt when Jim Croce died in a plane accident and my regrets that all the songs to come were never heard.

I can still feel the Alabama rain
Pouring within me
Just as it did the first time your clouds appeared
Celebrated clouds that invited the world to listen
Clouds that brought the early summer showers
Showers that flooded the earth within me
Transparent drops that trickled upon the ground
Glistening in apparel...standing in puddles
Until the fertile ground opened its arms
Nourishing the spirit
Growing, sprouting, becoming in someone else
What you can no longer be
Tell me the secrets...
I listen to the pines that whisper and whine
I listen to the singing birds and the croaking toads

I listen for my name
But they were your friends
And nature revealed her secrets to you
She sat and spoke to you
The melody was the wind
And your words traveled upon it
Carrying the cold that slapped my face
Holding the heat that hovered above my head
Sweat dripping from my brow as I faced the wind
The wind that you painted with a fiery red
Your rainbow is painted upon a charcoal disc
A promise that you will never leave
Your life is still spinning... spinning...
I hear your voice in the needle
Forever sewing the song
Creating the clothes that others will wear
Embroidered with the silver that lines the clouds
Crocheted with softness
Though you lie still and stagnate in the silence
I am moved
For your song is written on my heart
And the only ghost that haunts me is the sound I never heard

Nicholson and the Reverend Billy Graham at Graham's home,
Montreat, North Carolina. March 22, 2013.

22

ALL I EVER WANT TO BE

Then God said, "Let us make mankind in our image, in our likeness."
GENESIS 1:26, NIV

I wrote this song in college in 1982 as an attempt to express my desire to be more like Christ. It was a way to sing about my ultimate goal to reflect the attributes and qualities of His love. My sole desire was to be made into His image and likeness.

I want to be humble
Quiet in spirit
Confident enough to overcome
But wise enough to fear it
Patient in the midst of trial
Yet anxious to become Your child
Forever
I want to be emptied
Drained of all my ways
Yet filled with everything You are
And everything You say
Content with walking in the light
Yet ever searching for the night
In me
I want to be buried
Covered in Your ways
Yet risen in Your lasting love
Until the final day
Kind to all of those who are near
Gentle, honest, and sincere
Just to find a way to share

Let me serve you
Wash your feet
Laugh with you in victory
And cry in your defeat
The answer's yes before you ask
Because my God is in control
And I want to love Him with my heart, mind, and soul
Clothe the naked
Feed the hungry
Even take away my money
Give my dollars to the poor to make me rich
Return a favor, turn my cheek
In everything I do I seek
His will
But most of all just let me love
I guess you know that's why I'm here
I took my life awhile ago and stuck it on a shelf
Where you could see
That all I really ever want to be
Is Jesus living deep inside of me.

23

YOU ARE THE KEEPER OF YOUR HEART

Above all else, guard your heart, for everything you do flows from it.
PROVERBS 4:23, NIV

I wrote this poem in 1982 while in college. It focuses on the protection of one's heart. We are its keeper and we must guard and protect it from harm and ruin. We decide whether our heart is a home or a prison.

You are the keeper of your heart
A home or a prison in which you live
The key is your will
Directing the comfort or confinement that you choose
My love can only be invited
To sleep in your home or pace in your prison
For Love makes a home
And selfishness a prison
A true desire to give will open the door
But the door that lies broken
When repaired by Time will only close again
The steel bars are slammed shut
The vibrating and hollow sound of steel upon steel
Relentlessly echoes in the long, vacant hall of the soul
Only to become a nightmare of forgotten freedom
The captive's hands cling to the bars within
Screaming to be released
Even though the key lies within reach

Like the rose, a crown of love that sits majestically upon the vine
As I passed, 'tis not enough to share the beauty, but to possess it
All that the rose is can be shared within a touch

Its lingering fragrance I can smell

Its red velvet petals I can see

The rose acknowledges my attention and is aware of my attraction

All that it is offers its love in return

Yet the illusion evades me

It is not enough to share love, but to hold love

To embrace it as one's own

To possess and carry with me what others could have enjoyed

No thought of sharing

I must have it for my own

As I ripped the rose from its home

I paid no attention to the blood that ran down my arm

This pain meant little to me

In the light of my new possession

I locked it inside my heart

Beauty in a prison

Then I ran and ran until I fell from fatigue

I slept soundly with my prisoner

Until I awakened

Awakened to find the red velvet petals had wilted into a fragile, brown memory

All that is left is to find a place to preserve the lessons learned

Between the aging pages of the dusty volumes that sit silently upon my shelf

Lays the remembrance of what I could not own

You are the keeper of your heart

A home or a prison in which you live.

Master, have mercy

aw *them*. He said
ow yourselves to
so it was that as
ere cleansed.
em, when he saw
ed, returned
glorifi

we
en
?
t any
ory to

him,
th has ma

Kingdom

vas asked by t
kingdom of Go
swered them and
of God does not
ion;
say, 'See here!'
ideed, *b*the king-
in you."
o the disciples,
e when you will
of the days of
id you will not

ll say to you,
k there!' Do not
ow *them*.
ing that flashes
r heaven shines
der heaven, so
will be in His

st suffer many
ed by this gen-

14 *a*Lev. 13:1–
59; 14:1–32;
Matt. 8:4;
Luke 5:14
15 *a*Luke 5:25;
18:43
16 *a*2 K

*d*Noah, so it wil
of the Son
27 "Th

27 *a*Gen.
16
*b*Gen. 7:19
28 *a*Gen. 19
29 *a*Gen. 19:1
24, 29; 2 Pet.
2:6, 7
30 *a*[Matt.
16:27]; 1 Cor.
1:7; [Col. 3:4;
2 Thess. 1:7];
1 Pet. 1:7;
4:13; 1 John
2:28
31 *a*Matt.
24:17, 18;
Mark 13:15

2
2
b[
c[G
*d*1 P

t
ge

33 *a*Ma
John 12:
4:17] 1O

SONGS

These songs are like my children. Each one conceived in my heart, nurtured and loved as my own creation. Watching them grow in love and mystically engage with others has been a joyful experience. Just like my children, these songs will be my legacy. They will still be heard when I lie down in silence. Their fragrance will linger when I walk out the door and the scent of truth will surround the lives of those I love for generations to come. My songs... my legacy... *my own backyard*.

Chapters 24 - 37 are unrecorded songs.

Chapters 38 - 64 are recorded songs.

All songs and videos for "My Own Backyard" are featured on the **dannynicholson.com** website.

24

JUST AS LONG AS I HAVE YOU IN A SONG

A friend loves at all times,
and a brother is born for adversity.
PROVERBS 17:17, NIV

Pete Williams was my roommate in college. We were the best of friends.
Pete was on the track team with me running every workout. We ate
cheeseburgers late at night at Mama's. We played guitars all night long.
He was even with me the first night I met Debra, my wife. As he prepared
to transfer to another college, I wrote him this send-off song as a sad
goodbye to a friend who made so many wonderful memories. It is a song of
friendship and holds all the great times we shared.

I've waited and I've watched
And it's time for you to fly
Southern Winds are calling you home
So I guess I'll have to say goodbye
So long, now that your heart's where it belongs
Just thought I'd place the love we shared within a song
There are lots of memories in this simple song I sing
And every time I play this song
I hope it will bring me back to you
For awhile so that my heart can wear your smile
Just thought I'd place the love we shared with in a song
What good is your song if you're going away?
Within this melody I know you'll stay within my touch
And I'll love you just as much
And as long as I have you in a song
Just as long as I have you in a song

Love something feel inside
Something I just can't hide
Something I Know I've found - in You

And you - loved me enough to die
Blood dripping from your hands
Fell on a heart that was so dry.

Now something just overflows
Living water quenched my soul
All because I've found a home
in You.

Love is mine Because of you
Because of love I Know you li

"The Home I Found in You," 1982.
Original handwritten lyrics.

25

THE HOME I FOUND IN YOU

Remain in me, as I also remain in you. No branch can bear fruit by itself;
it must remain in the vine. Neither can you bear fruit unless you remain in me.
JOHN 15:4, NIV

This is one of the first songs I wrote in college in 1982. It was never recorded, but I sang it in coffee house concerts early on. It is a definition of love and what love does. It describes love as a home that I found, a home I was longing for. It seems early in my songwriting the simplicity of my heart was revealed in these feeble attempts to describe the spirit and emotion of my inner soul. It may not be a commercial success, but it sure holds the true feelings of my thoughts on how God's love is the home we are all looking for in this world.

Love...something I feel inside
Something I just can't hide
Something I know I found in You
And you loved me enough to die
Blood dripping from Your hands
Fell on a heart that was so dry
And now love seems to overflow
Living water quenched my soul
Don't you know I found a home in You
Love is mine because of You
And because of love I know
You live inside of everything I do
Because of Love I found a Home in You
Your love's in me as I live in You
Your wall's around my heart
Gave me a brand new start
And You built me an open door

Laid down the golden floors
Then painted my heart brand new
Don't You know I found a Home in You
Are you standing out in the cold
Your world about to fold
No one to run home to
Maybe sitting there in your Heaven all alone
Watching the world pass by
Laughing while they die
Well, I know God's sick and tired
Of the faces that we wear
Forgotten smiles and painted hearts
Does anybody care?
Does anybody care?
Love...something I feel inside
Something I just can't hide
Something I know I found in You
Don't You know I found a Home in You

                    D
A candle glowing inside of me
                D'
A wind is blowing its time to be
     G   A
Or the breathes breaths will take my flame away
    G   A   D
I better spread his love today

         D
The flame thats in me forever lives
           D
But if I dow ot share what our it give
        G   A   D
to the people in the valley that are cold
                    A   D
The time iswear the fire grows old

        C Darkening   G
I in the Winter world the only fire
                    E B
that warms your soul is the one he placed in
you
           C
And from the place thats always inside
   4 is love   F
take A spark and neve r hide the spark he
         C
places in you brave new

"I Should Have Spread His Love Today," 1981.
Original handwritten lyrics.

26

I SHOULD HAVE SPREAD HIS LOVE TODAY

*When Jesus spoke again to the people, he said, "I am the light of the world.
Whoever follows me will never walk in darkness, but will have the light of life."*
JOHN 8:12, NIV

This is one of the first songs I wrote in 1981. It is saying that life is short, and we should share God's love with everyone before our time is gone. When I first started playing and writing, there was a fresh desire to share with everyone the love that I had found. Those were very special days. The songs were a simple overflowing from my heart. Live and love with no regrets.

There's a candle glowing inside of me
A wind that's blowing...it's time to be

Or the breath I breathe will take my flame away
I better spread His love today

The flame that's in me, forever lives
But if I do not share, what will it give?

To the people in the valley down below
The time is near...the fire grows low

But in a darkening winter world
The only fire that warms your soul
Is the one He placed in you

So take this burning blaze inside
And with His love never hide the spark
He placed in you brand new

'Cause as a thief will come at night
And your spark will surely die
And your flame will fade away
And all that you can say
The candle glowing...yesterday

The blowing wind, well, it's taken it away
Yes, the breath He breathes has taken my flame away
Time is gone and ashes lay
I should have spread His love today

**Jamie Morphis, Lucy Brown, and myself at the
Darlington County Education Foundation program in 1998.**

Jamie and Lucy were friends and partners in many special projects
and together, we served others throughout the years.
This is the event where I presented the song, "Making a Difference."

27

MAKING A DIFFERENCE

He called a little child to him, and placed the child among them.
MATTHEW 18:2, NIV

This song was written for the initiation of the Darlington County Education Foundation in 1998. The foundation was created by my good friend, Jamie Morphis, to reward the teachers for their hard work and dedication to students. It was presented during one of our many programs held at the Darlington Raceway. On a personal note, I have watched my wife, Debra, give so much to her teaching profession through the years and I wanted to say how much I respect and appreciate all that she has done in her career to change the lives of students. Teachers make a difference.

I know it's hard for you to see the difference that you are making
When little hearts are breaking
And the days they seem so long
But you keep on because you know down in your heart
That a smile might be the spark that turns their silence into song
And you are making a difference
In every boy and girl
You're changing the heart of this great big world
And you're making a difference
Though sometimes it seems hard
You're changing your backyard
By going the distance
Tearing down fences
Making a Difference
Day after day, year after year
You nurture love and kindness
You comfort doubt and fear

You hold within your hand the future of the world
And the key that opens up the heart of every boy and girl
I know it's hard for you to keep believing that teaching makes
a difference everyday
Oh, just keep holding on, Oh, don't stop reaching
Cause I know you have touched one heart
that's why I'm here to say...here to say

28

THE BEST IS YET TO COME

Then the LORD replied: "Write down the revelation and make it plain on tablets
so that a herald may run with it.
HABAKUK 2:2, NIV

All of my dreams were born in the cradle of Charleston Southern University
(CSU) during my college days. I attended CSU from 1980-84. I received
a track scholarship, a degree in Communications, met my wife, Debra,
delivered our first child in the hospital across the street, began my music
ministry, and received my first job in higher education before I graduated.
All of these opportunities were realized during my college experience. That's
why I was proud to write "The Best is Yet to Come" with my good friend,
Rick Brewer, for the 35th anniversary of the college, and to celebrate the 15th
anniversary of President Jairy C. Hunter, Jr. in 1994.

Light the candles and close your eyes
Make a wish that we can realize
A wish of hope, a prayer of light
That can take away the darkness from the light
A wish where truth is more than empty words
A wish where compassion can be heard
Oh God, this is our prayer on this special day
Give us the strength and courage to find the way
As we celebrate your birthday and we raise the banner high
And we dedicate the future to a greater truth and light
As we focus on tomorrow we can't forget where we came from
'Cause on this special day we know that the best is yet to come
Press on and be determined 'cause your destiny's at hand
You were born for a purpose to help the world to understand
That intellect and knowledge are only tools used in vain
If they're not dedicated to the power of His name

As we celebrate your birthday and we raise the banner high
We dedicate the future to a greater truth and light
As we focus on tomorrow we can't forget where we came from
'Cause on the special day we know that the best is yet to come
So Happy Birthday to you
And may you always be true
Light the candles and close your eyes
And make a wish that we can realize
A wish of hope, a prayer of light
That can take away the darkness from the night

29

LONNIE LOU'S LULLABY

How priceless is your unfailing love, O God!
People take refuge in the shadow of your wings.
PSALM 36:7, NIV

This lullaby was written for the daughter of two very close friends, Eddy
and Angie Thomas. She is a princess. I remember praying that God would
protect her and make her an instrument of His love. "Lonnie Lou" was the
nickname we gave Caroline when she was a little girl, and this song was
created as a wish for her happiness in God's love.

LONNIE LOU'S LULLABY

Is a wish your dreams will fly
To the mountains – Oh so high
And sail the deep blue sea
Land upon a distant shore
Where only grace and peace endure
And God will keep you evermore
In His loving hands
And I pray you give your heart
To the One above
Until that time that God will keep you
In His hands of love
Lonnie Lou's Lullaby
Is a song I sang one night
When I was dreaming of your life
And all I want for you
That you will shine your little light
Across the darkness of the night
And show the world that Love is just

A simple prayer away
How I pray that you'll give your heart
To the One above
Until that time that God will keep you
In His hands of Love
Lonnie Lou's Lullaby
Is a heartfelt prayer
As I kiss you good night
I'll leave you in His care
I believe He'll keep you child
From the raging storm
Shelter you from the cold
Keep you safe and warm
In that place you'll give your heart
To the One above
Then you'll find that you will be
In His Hands of Love
Lonnie Lou's Lullaby
Is a dream that you will fly
To the mountains – Oh so high
And sail the deep blue sea.

30

CAN YOU REALLY TOUCH LOVE?

Now faith is confidence in what we hope for
and assurance about what we do not see.
HEBREWS 11:1, NIV

Everything that is truly powerful and sacred is invisible. We cannot see the wind, but it moves the trees; nor the Spirit; but it moves the soul. Love is the same way. We can't really see it or touch it; but Love is there. The problem is that we try to touch Love and call it something we can see. But as soon as we try to touch it in the physical world, it is gone. What man calls love will fade away and can never be held or possessed. What God calls Love lasts forever, and though we cannot touch it, we know that it is there and lasts, forever. I wrote this song in 1984. It reminds me of a Dan Fogelberg piece with the minor chords. It resembles the sound of songs from his "Innocent Age" album which is one of my all-time favorite pieces of creative work in music.

Some people build their world within the rushing wind
And tumble in the turmoil of losing love again
And heart shaped leaves that once knew spring
Unsnap themselves to find the coldness of the autumn air
In love they left behind
Tell me does the moment last forever
Does passion really speak?
Or is it just a fading voice that turns the strong to weak?
And as we stand there hand in hand
And we look into the stars up above
Tell me this...Can you really touch love?
All alone they sit and hold the memories that are gone
Of holding hands on summer sands while someone sang their song
And love that grew with sun and rain
And nearly touched the sky
Are wilted memories of fun and pain
And smiles that made them cry

31

THIS IS MY DREAM FOR YOU

A wife of noble character who can find? She is worth far more than rubies.
PROVERBS 31:10, NIV

Addison Wooten is Debra's niece. She is a beautiful young lady and she has been our "baby girl" ever since she was born. I was asked to sing at her dedication service and then again at her baptism. I decided to write this song to encourage my "baby girl" to follow the ways of God. My dream for her is to become a godly lady and to find her identity in His love. This song can serve as a dedication for any young girl to live the life of faith and be committed to His principles.

Where in the world can my baby girl find riches beyond all her dreams?
Where in the world can diamonds and pearls be replaced
by the love that You bring?
Tell me where in the world can my baby girl make all of her dreams come true?
It comes from the love that's found up above
And this is my dream for You
This is my dream for You.
Where in the world can the flag be unfurled like peace blowing in the wind?
Where in this life can anger and strife be replaced with a Love that's within?
Tell me where in the world can my baby girl make all of her dreams come true
It comes from the love that's found up above
And this is my dream for You
This is my dream for you.
So go down into the water and wash away all of your sins
And rise to the light in the midst of the night
And begin your new life again
Begin your new life again.

Where in your heart can you find a start that washes away all of your past?
Where in your soul can the story be told with a love that will always last?
Tell me where in the world can my baby girl make all of her dreams come true
It comes from the love that's found up above
And this is my dream for you
This is my dream for you.

32

SUMMERTIME AGAIN

I thank my God every time I remember you.
PHILIPPIANS 1:3, NIV

I met Shannon Tanner during my freshman year in college. He was sitting on the sidewalk between the dorms singing and playing his guitar. We became instant friends. Shannon is the kind of guy that would give you the shirt off his back.

Shannon is a musician by trade. In the summer, he sings and plays in Hilton Head, South Carolina, where his family lives. But in the winter, he plays in Veil, Colorado. Leaving his family every year is hard, but that's the life of a music man.

I wrote this song for him in 2002 at 26 Olde Canal Loop in Pawley's Island, South Carolina when he was leaving for his winter journey. I called him and shared these words on the phone. It was my way of supporting him while he was away from his family. It was a prayer for him to stay strong until summertime comes again.

It's Thanksgiving in Colorado
And I woke up all alone
The cold November wind is blowing
So I called you on the phone

We talked about the time we shared
And the memories that we hold
The sound of your sweet, sweet voice
Will keep me warm until I'm home

Oh the thought of you warms my heart
Though I'm cold and all alone
All the times we left behind

Will keep me warm until I'm home
And it's good to know in winter time
You will always be my friend
And that will keep me warm
'Til it's summertime again.

So place those memories in the fireplace
Just enough to warm my soul
I'll just pull them out one more time
'Cause my heart is frozen cold

As the flames rise and dance inside
I pray warmth will see me through
And keep me holding on 'til the sun will shine
And all my dreams come true

Oh yes, seasons come and seasons go
But summertime is when
I come home to Carolina
And hold my dreams again

Yes, the thought of you warms my heart
Though I'm cold and all alone
All the times we left behind
Will keep me warm until I'm home
And it's good to know in wintertime
You always have a friend
And that will keep me warm 'til
It's summertime again

33

IN THE NAME OF LOVE

These things I remember as I pour out my soul
PSALM 42:4, NIV

I was asked to read the names of soldiers who gave their lives during the Iraq war in October 2011. The memorial service was held at the Student Center on the campus of Carson-Newman University. As I entered the small room, I noticed there were only two people besides me. One was a gentleman reading the names and the other was a soldier waiting to read. When the soldier began to read, I was the only one in the room. When I stood to call out the names, I was the only one in the room. I was moved by the meaning of the moment as I heard the names echoing across the empty room. I thought of the faceless names, their families and loved ones. When I finished, I wrote down these words in honor of their silent sacrifice for my freedom - "You will not be forgotten - In the Name of Love."

One by one I called out their names
The sound fell to silence 'cause no one remained
But I know that He heard me
'Cause He lost a son
To a war He created and had already won
One by One they lowered them down
No one was there when they were placed in the ground
No one remembered 'cause no one was there
But God as my witness I heard them singing this prayer
In the name of Love
In the name of Love
You will not be forgotten
In the name of Love
Your name will be spoken by the Father above
He'll call out your name
In the name of Love

34

MY HEART TURNED TO STONE

I will give you a new heart and put a new spirit in you;
I will remove from you your heart of stone and give you a heart of flesh.
EZEKIEL 36:26, NIV

This is one of those songs that fell out of my imagination. It speaks to how heartbreak can make your heart turn to stone. Sometimes we are hurt so badly that we close off the world and our heart turns cold. Broken relationships have a way of tearing our trust in others apart. Lesson learned: We have to trust God and know that He is the only One that will always be there. Nothing on this earth lasts forever so we cannot depend on that which does not last. I wrote this in 2011, when we first moved into our home in Morristown, Tennessee.

I didn't say I was leaving
I didn't stay I would stay
Just give me something to believe in
Like you said yesterday.
Your lies are forgiven
But the giving is gone
And I sank to the bottom
When my heart turned to stone.
I remember the first time
When you called out my name
And I knew in that moment
I'd never be the same.

Sweet summer sunshine
I would never forget
Turned into a winter
Full of regrets.

I remember, oh, the fireworks in July
Glowing embers on the beach that slowly died.
By September, you left me standing all alone
Without a warning in the morning
My heart turned to stone
I picked up a pebble
And I skipped it cross the water.
It made me remember
How we spent our last quarter
In the jukebox that evening
When I played our last song
And we danced until midnight
And my heart turned to stone.

35

STOP LOVING ME AND START LOVING YOU

If I speak in the tongues of men or of angels, but do not have love,
I am only a resounding gong or a clanging cymbal.
If I have the gift of prophecy and can fathom all mysteries and all knowledge,
and if I have faith that can move mountains, but do not have love, I am nothing.
If I give all I possess to the poor and give over my body to hardship that
I may boast, but do not have love, I gain nothing.
I CORINTHIANS 13:1, NIV

I have always struggled with the meaning of Love. Like all human beings, I know intellectually that love is about sacrifice. But when it comes to living it out, I fail miserably. That's because we love ourselves more than we love others. True love is loving others more than ourselves. This song explores dreams, romance, and memories. It moves back and forth between human love and divine love. The final thought in the bridge is that "love is not something that reflects my needs, but a window that reveals what is broken and bleeds." In other words, it is a selfless act that releases God/others from what we want them to be and focuses on the brokenness. I'm going to *Stop Loving Me and Start Loving You*. I wrote this in 2011 while I was commuting back and forth to Carson-Newman University.

I'm going to stop loving me and start loving you
Surrender my pride and submit to what's true
Quit trying to make you just like me
Release you from prison and let you go free
The promise of Eden is where our hearts were deceived
But sacrifice's womb is where love was conceived
We were born to be different, alive and true
I'm going to stop loving me and start loving you.
We are all different like the stars up above
And differences define the meaning of love
I just love myself in all that I do

Until I stop loving me and start loving you.
My dreams are a widow who lost her first love
Lingering in sorrow, searching above
Waiting for someone to rescue my blues
I'm going to stop loving me and start loving you.
Dreaming of romance, a candlelight dance
Just fading memories that don't have a chance
Of filling my heart the way that you do
I'm going to stop loving me and start loving you.
I guess these memories have been my old friends
Until I wake up and start it all over again
Yesterday's gone and I've paid all my dues
That's why I'll stopped loving me and start loving you.
Love's not a mirror reflecting my needs
But a window revealing what's broken and bleeds
I'm going to stop loving me and start loving you
Surrender my pride and submit to what's true
Quit trying to make you just like me
Release you from prison and let you go free.

Nicholson's dad, Billy, and sons, Taylor and Bryson.
DeDe's Beach House in Garden City, South Carolina, 2003.

36

GOODBYE OLD FRIEND

Lift your eyes and look to the heavens: Who created all these?
He who brings out the starry host one by one, and calls them each by name.
Because of his great power and mighty strength, not one of them is missing.
ISAIAH 40:26, NIV

It was a December night in 2011. I stepped out on the porch for one last look at the stars before I said good night. When I finally laid down to sleep, I could still see the stars in the sky. My dad had just come home from the hospital after a month and we were thankful that he would be home for Christmas. He was on my mind and heart when I went out to stare into the sky. For some reason I saw him in the stars. The next morning I woke up with this song in my heart. I will see you in the stars again real soon.

You never really said that you were leaving
But I knew when I looked into your eyes
This would be the last time I would see you
So I kissed you gently and said goodbye.
Goodbye, old friend
It's been a good one
Now you can go and dance around the moon
Tell Grandpa and the family that we miss them
I will see you in the stars again real soon
I will see you in the stars again real soon.
Last night we gathered on the front porch
And we sang to the stars up above
And I swear I heard your voice come down from Heaven
It was singing that familiar song of Love.

Goodbye, old friend
It's been a good one

Now I can see you dancing around the moon
Keep singing with the angels up in Heaven
I will see you in the stars again real soon
I will see you in the stars again real soon.

Sometimes the stars up in the sky
Put on a show....what a beautiful sight
And when I finally say good night
I think of you.
I think of you.
Goodbye, old friend
It's been a good one
Now I can see you dancing around the moon
Keep singing with the angels up in heaven
I will see you in the stars again real soon
I will see you in the stars again real soon.

37

FOUR LETTER WORDS

The words of wisemen are like goads, and masters of these collections
are like well driven nails; they are given by one Shepherd.
ECCLESIASTES 12:11, NIV

I wrote this song on Christmas Day 2017 when we had only been at Connie
Maxwell for a few months. It was a gift on Christmas. It came to me while
I was riding in the car. I thought of how we think of four letter words as
bad words. Then the words - love, kind, good, true, soul, star, wind, moon,
song, holy, mama, life, dawn, rose appeared in my mind and I thought,
"Four Letter Words" are more than bad words. They are words that give life,
manifest beauty, and make life worth living.

CHRISTMAS 2017

I grew up listening to my Daddy
Making Mama cry with four letter words
He said them with a whole lot of passion
And I remember every single one I heard

He said them when the sun was gently rising
They shined from the front porch filled with light
He picked red ones from the garden in the morning
He painted them in the stars at night

(chorus)
He said, "Love... your neighbor.
Always be good, kind, and true
And Love... will bring you favor
Hidden in the little things you say and do."

And Hold... your dear Mama
While remembering the lessons that you've heard
Life will unfold
And the story will be told
Written down in Four Letter Words.

Four letter words are nothing really fancy
Just poetry for the common man
He sang them in a song
And on one early dawn
He prayed them while he held me in his hands

He said them at my high school graduation
He walked them on my holy wedding day
And on that precious morn
when my little boy was born
He took his little hand and showed the way

(chorus)
He said, "Love....your neighbor.
Always be good, kind, and true.
And life will bring you favor
Hidden in the little things you say and do."
And Hold....your dear Mama
While remembering the lessons that you've heard
Life will unfold
And the story will be told
Written down in Four Letter Words

(bridge)
One word was on the head board of his tombstone
Its the only one he cared to scribble down
As we carved it in real deep

And laid him down to sleep
I still could hear that sweet familiar sound

(chorus)
Four Letter Words... whispering in the pine
Four Letter Words in the moon and star that shine
Four Letter Words in the rose that will bloom
Four Letter Words in the soul of me and you.

The Cross He Gave To Me

This guitar was given to me
By the God who made the mountain and tree
Cut and shaped for a purpose to be
An instument of wood for Thee

Though it happened two thousand years ago
He played a song to help the world to see
That the instrument that He played upon
Made the song that set me free
And this old guitar is the Cross He Gave to me.

These silver strings their made out of steel
They remind me of hard driven spikes
That became a part of the Cross
Made the sound of supreme sacrifice
When they nailed them in His hands
I can feel it when I play
And every time I touch these strings
I remember the price He paid.

Though it happened two thousand years ago
He played a song to help the world to see
That the instrument He played upon
Made the song that set me free
And this old guitar is the Cross He gave to me.

The song still remains and its dipped in the blood
What the Cross or the spikes could not give
Cause the man on the Cross with the spikes in His hands
Chose to give His life so you could live
I can't die to save you but I sure can sing this song
And play the Cross He gave me and sing of His perfect love.

He played an everlasting song
When He died on the Cross a long, long time ago
And I pray that you've heard through this old guitar
Of how He loved you so.

This old guitar's The Cross He Gave To Me.

Original typed copy
of the song "The Cross
He Gave to Me."

The image to the left is a
my Yamaha guitar captured
during a photo session for
the "Heart of Love" Album.

Most of my songs were
written on this instrument,
a gift from a friend in
high school.

38

THE CROSS HE GAVE TO ME

And so it was with me, brothers and sisters.
When I came to you, I did not come with eloquence or human wisdom as I
proclaimed to you the testimony about God. For I resolved to know nothing
while I was with you except Jesus Christ and him crucified. I came to you in
weakness with great fear and trembling. My message and my preaching were
not with wise and persuasive words, but with a demonstration of the Spirit's
power, so that your faith might not rest on human wisdom, but on God's power.
I Corinthians 2:1-5, NIV

In the summer of 1982, my freshman year in college, I came home to
Hartsville, South Carolina to relax, run, and play the guitar. I had just
started playing guitar, and there was a burning desire in me to write a song.
I had been moved by music always, but now I wanted to sing something
that would move others. I only knew the basic chords and had not really
practiced a lot but I wanted to say something with my guitar, something
that really mattered. It was all consuming, and I was committed to writing
a song. I remember it was a blistering hot day. I wanted to be alone, to have
some time to think and play.

In my own backyard, my dad had a workshop. It was the place where he
worked and kept all his tools. I made my way to the workshop and closed
the door. It was hot outside and the workshop had no air conditioning. I
was burning up, and sweat was pouring down my face, but I was unaffected.
I was going to write a song. I sat and played for a long time only to be
frustrated by my inability to come up with something meaningful. I placed
my guitar up against a table and sat on the stool with my head in my hands.
As I looked up, I saw the guitar was angled with the back towards me. It was
like a mirror on the back, and I looked down and saw my reflection. In the
silence, I thought, "that's my problem. I am trying to reflect me through this
instrument." Then I began to see my old guitar as something completely
different. Music was not made to reflect me. It was made to reflect God's
love. In that moment, I saw the wood on the guitar as the cross, the strings
as the spikes in His hands, and the song as the blood that flows from the
two. This is the first real song I ever wrote. I began my journey to glorify
God with my music. It has always served as a reminder of what music is

all about and it laid the foundation for all that I said in music through the years. God gave me this song. I am thankful that I wrote it in my own backyard.

Song 1

This guitar was given to me
By the God who made the mountain and tree
Cut and shaped for a purpose to be
An instrument of wood for Thee.
Though it happened two thousand years ago
He played a song to help the world to see
That the instrument He played upon
Made the song that set me free
This old guitar was the Cross He gave to me.

These silver strings they're made out of steel
They remind me of hard driven spikes
That became a part of the Cross
Made the sound of supreme sacrifice
When they nailed them in His hands.
I can feel it when I play
And every time I touch these strings
I remember the price he paid.

Now the song still remains and it's dipped in the blood
What the Cross or the spikes could not give
'Cause the man on the Cross with the spikes in His hands
Chose to give His life so you could live
And I can't die to save you but I sure can sing this song
And play the cross He gave me
And sing of His perfect love.

Visual representation of "The Portrait of the Crying Clown.
A gift from friend, Gary Conway.

39

THE PORTRAIT OF THE CRYING CLOWN

For the LORD searches every heart and understands
every motive behind the thoughts.
1 CHRONICLES 28:9, NIV

"The Portrait of the Crying Clown" was written in 1989 in the trailer
that Debra and I lived in on Stall Road in Charleston, South Carolina.
I remember struggling with God in my heart and truly living out the
Christian life. This song came to me at the piano one day and became an
autobiographical expression of my life's story. I had always been like a clown
wanting attention and causing everyone around me to laugh, but down
deep inside I was crying out for peace and understanding. This song brought
me to a place of surrender and understanding that there is only One in the
audience, and that true laughter and freedom come from the heart.

Song 2

Long, Long time ago I traveled in a three ringed circus show
Sweeping spotlights from a dark and dusty floor
As I made the people laugh I cried for more
But the tears they never could erase a perfect painted face
And it was all a masquerade

'Cause every time the lights went down the smile would fade
And it wasn't even worth the pennies paid
To see an actor just act upon a stage
'Cause what they were after was the laughter of the heart
The only missing part

And now the Crying Clown
He travels to the towns
Giving back to them the smile he never found

'Cause through the aging years buried under all those tears
He finally found the only missing part
The Laughter of the Heart.

After all those years here I stand within the circus of my fears
The seats are empty, there's not a single soul in sight
But in the center ring I stand laughing in the light
You see I finally found the most important part
The Laughter of the Heart.

danny nicholson

heart of love

"Heart of Love" album cover.

40

HEART OF LOVE

Nor will people say, 'Here it is,' or 'There it is,'
because the kingdom of God is within you.
LUKE 17:21, NIV

One night in 1984, my college roommates and I were watching the *Wizard of Oz*. I have always had a fascination with this epic movie because it reminds me of my childhood. As a child, I used to wait all year long for the *Wizard of Oz* to come on. I don't think I ever missed it. It's that old familiar story about finding home; but I never get tired of it, and noticeably no one else does either.

That night, as the movie concluded, the line that Dorothy says at the end jumped out at me. I don't know how to explain it, but it felt like the statement was just for me. She said, "If I ever go looking for home again, I won't look any further than my own backyard because if it is not there, I never lost it to begin with." I was struck. I excused myself and went to my piano (which my dad gave to me) and sat down to write "Heart of Love." This moment defined the north star in my life. Happiness is not out there far away. Happiness is in your heart. If you quit searching for Oz, you will find everything in your own backyard. Not long after I wrote this song, I formed a band. We became known as Heart of Love because every time we played, we shared the story of how happiness is found in one's own backyard. "There is no place like home."

Song 3

Sometimes it seems like we all live in Kansas
Searching for love in the sky
Looking for somewhere over the rainbow
Hoping that one day we will find
A pot of gold or maybe a wizard
Makes all our dreams come true
When that somewhere over the rainbow
Is found in the heart of you

So keep holding on to your dreams even though they seem to hide
We look so far away to find what is deep inside
So keep holding on to the things that your heart has been dreaming of
'Cause somewhere over the rainbow is found in a Heart of Love.
You might be a lion who needs some courage
Or a tin man who needs a heart
Or a little girl just like Dorothy
Looking for a place to start.
You can travel down the yellow brick road
And find all your dreams on your own
But when you get there you'll just turn around
And say there's really no place like home.
There's no place like home
There's no place like home
There's no place like home

Nicholson as a child. 1964

41

AS A CHILD

All your children will be taught by the Lord,
and great will be their peace.
Isaiah 54:13, NIV

As a child, I vividly remember laying on the grassy hill in my front yard and staring at the stars in the sky. My memory is bathed in a fresh innocence that only children have. My childhood was laced with many "holy moments" of being immersed in my dreams and pretending I was an astronaut or singing on stage. That's one of the wonders of childhood, the creative imagination untouched by the world. This song touches on a deep well of fascination and always transports me back to that place of holy desire and longing. The imagery of connecting the stars or creating an angel out of snow are recollections of youthful bliss I shall never forget. Simon and Garfunkel once wrote in a song called "Bookends," this beautiful line,

"Preserve your memories - they are all that's left you."

Song 4

As a child I could be anything in the twinkling of an eye
A cowboy or a hero or a bird that simply flies
I could turn into a fireman on a Sunday afternoon
Or suddenly an astronaut heading towards the moon.
A star in front of thousands as a record slowly plays
In a blue jean pair of trousers, a conductor on a train
Would carry me to paradise where I could be a King
And I'd just spend my time living out my dreams.

And as a child I was like that though it seems so long ago
I could make an angel out of the cold and bitter snow
As I look back I can clearly see that the toys are still the same

The only difference is the way I play the game.
Oh take me back unto the days when I could stare into the night
And the only thing that I could see were the little twinkling lights
And the stars were just a draw by number pad within my sky
And I'd spend my time connecting dreams and never wonder why.

42

OLD HYMNS

Speak to one another with psalms, hymns and spiritual songs.
Sing and make music in your heart to the Lord.
EPHESIANS 5:19, NIV

This song was written in my dorm room in 1983 as a tribute to the old
hymns I sang in church as a young boy. I remember watching the hometown
choir stand to sing the old songs that stirred my heart. *Amazing Grace*,
Blessed Assurance, and *How Great Thou Art* are hymns that brought back my
childhood memories of sitting in church singing songs of faith and love. It's
hard to go back to those holy moments but every time I sing this song,
I remember.

Song 5

I was just a young boy when I first heard them old songs
I was standing with my mother and I was trying to sing along
I'd tip toe to catch a verse or two to help my little heart to see
That this man they call Jesus was living in a melody
And the Old Hymns, they do it best for me
I once was lost but now I see
His loving face when I sing "Amazing Grace"
He stole my heart when I heard "How Great Thou Art"
Blessed Assurance Jesus is mine
Here's to the Old Hymns...Forever in Time
Well, I guess I'm a little bit older now but I'll never forget the days
When the hometown choir would stand and sing those good old hymns of praise
And my little hands would tremble
As a tear fell to the floor
I heard Him inside knocking and I opened up the door.
And the Old Hymns, they do it best for me
I once was lost but now I see

His loving face when I sing "Amazing Grace"
He stole my heart when I heard "How Great Thou Art"
Blessed Assurance Jesus is mine
Here's to the Old Hymns...Forever in Time

43

DEAR JOHN

He will swallow up death forever.
The Sovereign Lord will wipe away the tears from all faces.
ISAIAH 25:8, NIV

John Lide was a friend of mine during my elementary, junior high, and high school years. We played basketball together, and I remember we always kidded him about his "big feet." In fact, we affectionately called him, *Feets*.

The friends you grow up with are always considered family in your life. John was a member of the family. I remember coming home during college break, and my mom meeting me at the door to announce that John had died. I was shocked. It was hard to believe that a friend of mine, who I considered family, had left the world at 25 years of age. My mom said that John was sitting on his bed in his dorm room at UNC - Chapel Hill and fell over dead. He had one shoe off and one shoe on when he died. In the middle of an ordinary moment, John left the world without a chance to say goodbye.

This was my goodbye song to John - a way of bringing closure to a deafening moment of uncertainty and pain. I guess I am not the only one who has lost someone they loved without saying goodbye. So, this is a personal testimony and tribute to a life that was gone too soon. It also brings a sense of urgency to love those around us and share our faith with everyone. Tomorrow is not promised. For years we closed our concert with this song in an attempt to share with others what I never had a chance to share with John. "Did you pray before you died or did you only try to fly, Dear John.

Song 6

Dear John, I haven't seen you in awhile
It seems that I have forgotten the beauty of your smile
I thought that we could sit around and fumble through the files
And mingle through the memories that were lost between the miles

Dear John

Dear John, I hear that you were leaving
Your distant destination was surprisingly deceiving
It slipped up on you like a friend
And tapped you on the back
No thought for preparation and no more time to pack

Dear John
Doesn't time slip away when you got so far to go?
Your exit came at twenty five and your curtains quietly closed
And you never really got the chance to see the final show
Dear John...I loved you so.

Dear John, such a silent goodbye
Did you ever really stop and ask the question why?
Or were you just a tight rope walker spiraling in the sky?
Did you pray before you died or did you only try to fly?

Dear John
Dear John, I sign this letter with my love
Though I don't know where to send it, You know what I'm speaking of
And I really wish you would have got the chance to see the show
Sometimes the curtains close before the actor even knows
Dear John

44

SILVER AND GOLD

Religion that God our Father accepts as pure and faultless is this:
to look after orphans and widows in their distress
and to keep oneself from being polluted by the world.
JAMES 1:27, NIV

This song was written in the summer of 1982 for Tootsie Mobley. Tootsie was a silver haired widow grandmother of Gennie Hunter in Hartsville, South Carolina, who had become a close friend through our visits in high school and college. I woke up on this summer morning and the song wrote itself as my heart desired to tell her how much she meant to me. I remember the first time I sang it to her. It was a moment. Then on the day of her funeral I sang it to her one last time. She had a heart of gold and I will always thank God for her friendship and love. She lives in this song.

Song 7

There's a picture that is sitting on the shelf within my soul
Of a beautiful lady, silver hair and heart of gold
And her smile is like the sunshine on an early summer's morn
And her heart is like the garden where the purest rose is born.
The flowers and the music are the reasons that she lives
She finds life within the simple things that only life can give
She always takes the time to smell the roses when she passes
'Cause she knows she's making memories, the only ones that last.

Silver hair and heart of gold on the picture of my soul
Time is new but love is old though the story is seldom told
There will always be a place where time cannot erase
The love and laughter that we hold
Silver and Gold

Just like the ocean the time we spend it comes and goes
So when I go home I stop by to see her heart of gold
And we talk about the good old times and we always laugh awhile

Just remembering the times we danced I begin to gently smile
Then suddenly I realize that the memories that I hold
Come from a beautiful lady
Silver hair and heart of gold

Debra and Danny Nicholson.
Top: Before their first prom in college, 1983.
Bottom: At the reflection pond in between classes at Charleston Southern University.

45

FOREVER

Husbands, love your wives, even as Christ also loved the church,
and gave Himself for it.
EPHESIANS 5:25, NIV

I met my wife, Debra, at 3:00 a.m. outside her dorm room window in 1982. Pete Williams, my college roommate, had enlisted me to sing, "I'm in the Mood for Love" to his girlfriend who was listening from her third floor window. After a few lines of the song, the light came on in the first floor window. Apparently, we had awakened someone from her sleep. The curtains parted and there before my very eyes was an angel. I walked towards the window to apologize for our rude late night serenade.

"It's 3:00 in the morning," she softly whispered.

"I am so sorry," I replied. Then I noticed that she did not close the window. We talked and after a few minutes, I finally found the courage to ask her if she would like to walk on the beach the next night. She agreed, and I ran to wake all of my friends to announce who I was going out with.

The next night we went to the beach for our first date on the Isle of Palms. We talked about our lives—she told me of the pain of losing Brian, her nephew, to leukemia, and I told her my testimony. We have been together ever since. On June 1, 1985, we were married in her hometown church in Nixville, South Carolina. I wrote this song for our wedding ceremony and sang it to her on the day I proposed. As a surprise I came out from behind a puppet stand in the sanctuary of the same church.

"Forever" is a song of my everlasting love for God and her. There may be trials and tribulations in marriage but God's Love overcomes every human circumstance. Just like our personally written vows stated, "I would rather die than love you more than God." God's love is "Forever" and so our love will be until the end of time.

Song 8

Well, it's time we made a change
Started to live our lives together
Started to be this way until forever comes
And it's not a long, long way
Until the end starts the beginning
Of a life that only dreams could understand.
So the time has finally come
And there you stand before me
Gazing in my eyes with all your love
And I felt you step inside
You made a home out of my prison
You brought the spring into the season of my soul.
Together...I found a way
To see the love you gave me
To turn the night into day
That forever...we will be
Together...Forever...you and me.
And as we chase the rising Son
And leave the night behind us
Hoping that the morning finds us here
In the light, Clinging to the sunshine
Burning beams of love within our hearts.

Nicholson's holding sons Taylor and Bryson's hands in a photo session for the "Heart of Love" Album.

46

BEFORE YOU WERE BORN

Before I formed you in the womb I knew you,
before you were born I set you apart;
I appointed you as a prophet to the nations.
JEREMIAH 1:5, NIV

This song was written at the birth of my first son, Taylor, in 1989. It is dedicated to both my sons in an attempt to explain the awesome feeling a dad has when his children come into this world. I remember being overwhelmed when I saw them for the first time.

Debra and I were amazed at their little hands and feet. The sound of their first cry when arriving was indescribable. No doubt it is one of the happiest days of our lives. Our sons were God's gift to us.

Song 9

Before you were born

Before you were formed in the heart of me

You were a part of me

And only God knows how I loved you then.

Even when I'd never held you tight

Or watched you sleep within the night

Or seen your mother's smile within your eyes

What a pleasant surprise

When you were born

I loved you more than words can say

Your little hands

Your simple ways

They opened the door to my heart

When you were born God blessed the day I heard the news.

My skies of gray and clouds of blue faded away

When you were born...When you were born
You came in with the sun
You brought the morning light
You stole away the darkness
A shining star within the night
You gave me everything that life is all about
You filled my empty heart and washed away my doubts.

47

A PICTURE OF HOME

"One thing I ask of the Lord, this is what I seek: that I may dwell in the House of the Lord all the days of my life, to gaze upon the beauty of the Lord and to seek Him in His temple."
PSALM 27:4, NIV

For many years, I travelled to concerts and returned home early in the morning. I always wanted to pray over my children each day and crawl into my own bed to go to sleep. One night as I entered our townhouse in Summerville, South Carolina, the wedding picture of my wife Debra caught my eye and heart. In the stillness of the morning, I was inspired to place these emotions in a song as I reflected on just how much her presence, my children, and our home meant to my life. This song brings to life the little things that give our life meaning: The fireplace, the wedding pictures, the white lace on her wedding dress that is stored in the attic, the rocking chair, a face in the window waving goodbye. This song is a picture of home.

Song 10

When I'm all alone chasing my dreams
Sometimes it seems such a waste to go on
'Cause late in the night, all my visions of flight seem to fall
All alone I would not trade all I own
For one thought of you or a picture of home
'Cause wrapped in the scrapbook of tears that I cry
Is a face in the window waving goodbye

Home, such a lovely place
More beautiful than all of the dreams I chase
Like the warmth of the fire in the old fireplace
Dancing around like a vision of grace
That's my home and I'll never erase

The little things chosen, times frozen in place
Like your soft golden hair, the white linen lace
Just a trace of the place I call home.

And when I go home
The welcome mat greets me at my front door
The easy chairs rocking and the rug on the floor
And the little hands reaching, wanting me more
Than those cold and lonely dreams that I chase
One day they'll die but I'll never erase
The light on the front porch, my children's embrace
Just a trace of the place I call home

48

CRY FOR THE PEOPLE

Blessed are those who mourn, for they will be comforted.
Matthew 5:4, NIV

During my college years, I sang at hundreds of concerts and retreats. One retreat I remember vividly was for a Baptist Student Union at the Citadel Beach house. After my presentation, I was asked why I so freely share my heartfelt emotions when I sing and speak. I was taken back by the question, and it caused me to evaluate my motives. I did not mean to use emotion as a manipulative tool, but an authentic, sincere manifestation of my heart and life. I thought and prayed for weeks about this moment before my response to this question came out in a song. The first line of the song is, "You ask me why I Cry for the People?" My answer follows.

This is the first song our band played together during a revival on the Charleston Southern campus. It still moves me every time I sing it. Crying is not a display of weakness; it is the rinsing and washing of one's spirit. Tears say what words will never find. I encourage others to reveal their compassion while ministering to the needs of people.

Song 11

You ask me why I cry for the people
Just look around you, the answer is so clear
They stand in the streets as we sing our songs in the steeple
Calling our freedom just an escape from our fears
Well, I don't understand how they live their lives in blindness
Calling our kindness just a game that we play
But what's really sad is that we leave them all behind us
Pretending that one day they'll find a way
We've got to cry...Cry for the people
We've got to try...Try while we can
To show them that life is more than just strife

Or wind blowing through empty steeples
It's a change in your heart that only will start
When love burns in the lives of God's people
Oh, when will we find our pride left behind?
And care enough to cry... cry for the people.
Don't get me wrong, there is no devotion
Where only emotion is ruler and king
But it seems in the kingdom we've made love so out of fashion
Forgetting compassion for the lost while we sing
What is our song and all of our learning?
If we are not yearning to love dying souls
And take love as a spark and find our hearts burning
To cry for the people or not live at all.

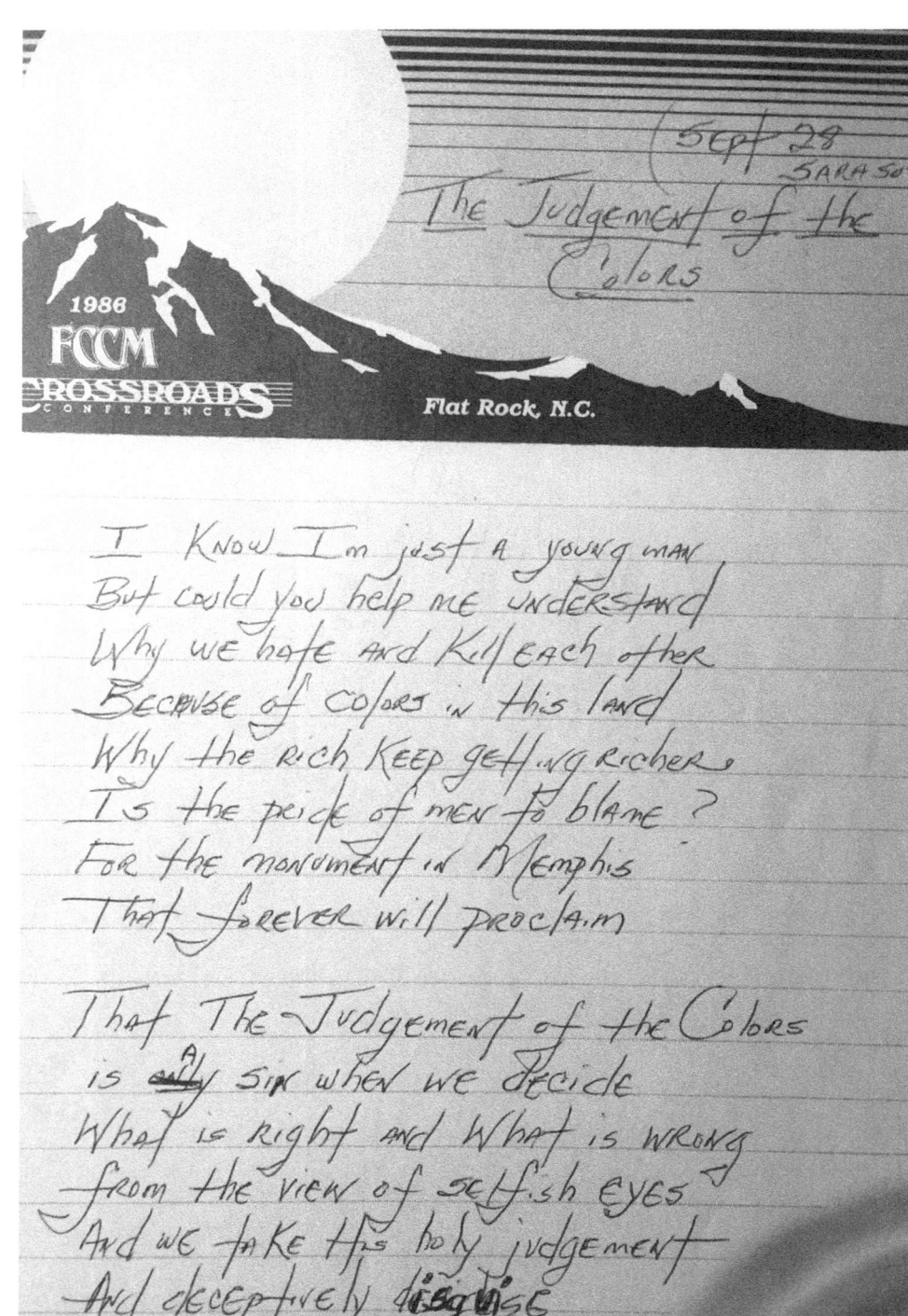

(Sept 28
SARASO,

The Judgement of the
Colors

I KNOW I'm just A young man
But could you help me UNDERSTAND
Why we hate And Kill EACH other
BECAUSE of COLORS in this land
Why the rich keep getting richer
Is the pride of men to blame?
For the monument in Memphis
That forever will proclaim

That The Judgement of the Colors
is only sin when we decide
What is right And What is wrong
from the view of selfish eyes
And we take this holy judgement
And deceptively disguise

"Judgement of the Colors." 1985.
Original handwritten lyrics.

178

49

JUDGMENT OF THE COLORS

You nullify the Word of God by your tradition that you have handed down.
MARK 7:13, NIV

During my first year out of college in 1985, I worked in the Admissions
Office of Charleston Southern University. My job required me to travel
a lot to recruit students. One morning, in a hotel room in Jacksonville,
Florida, I was watching TV and saw a recording of Martin Luther King,
Jr. giving his "I Have a Dream" speech. I remember being overcome with
emotion and writing down this song about the injustice of prejudice. It is
one of my personal favorites because it portrays the mercy and judgment
of God. Through the years, Kevin Jones, the band, and I have sung this song
hundreds of times, and I cannot remember a concert where the message
did not penetrate the hearts of those in attendance in an authentic way.
This song was a gift from God.

Song 12

Well, I know I'm just a young man

But could you help me understand

How we kill and hate each other because of colors in this land?

Why the rich keep getting richer, is the pride of man to blame?

For the monument in Memphis that forever will proclaim

That the judgment of the colors is only sin when we decide

What is right and what is wrong in the view of selfish eyes

We mistreat His holy judgment and deceptively disguise

The strength of love and freedom in the weakness of our lies, our lies.

Tell me who gave you the right to destroy a poor man's dream

To deprive a soul of freedom or to kill an honest king.

I think we're only drifting away from God's own plan

When we're the judge of colors within the heart of man

Well, we're all just broken crayons that are scattered across the earth

Red and yellow, black and white, In God's eyes we all were worth
The precious price of Jesus and our lives did not depend
On the church that we attended or the color of our skin.
But we turn our heads and walk away as a little black boy dies
And it seems our slumbering silent hearts will never realize
That we are held responsible and the reflection in his eyes
Showed the judgment of the colors was the reason that he died, he died.

I've got a picture
Of a world in the Son
Black and white people
Standing as one
Loving each other in the light hand and hand
While the walls that divide us no longer stand
Bring us together
Shine down from above
Color our canvas with a picture of love
With hope for tomorrow
Wash our sorrows away
Bring us together
Into the gray.

**Nicholson with Gene Cotton at his reunion concert
to raise money for "The Nicaragua Project."**

The guitar is a prized treasure of Nicholson's with signatures from
Gene Cotton, Marnie (his wife), and his original band.

50

I'VE SEEN A PICTURE

I saw heaven standing open and there before me was a white horse,
whose rider is called Faithful and True.
With justice He judges and makes war. His eyes are like blazing fire,
and on His head are many crowns.
He has a name written on Him that no one knows but He Himself.
REVELATION 19:11, NIV

The seed for this song was started on the first album, "In the Hands of God," with the ending chorus of "Judgment of the Colors." It was entitled, "Into the Grey." It was written as an a cappella chorus to bring hope and light to a world full of hate and prejudice. After recording it with Gene Cotton at *Creative Studios* in Nashville, Tennessee, he asked if he could write a song based on this chorus. It was a highlight moment for me to have him co-write a song.

"I've Seen a Picture" was rewritten to say that the song was not complete. It is a hopeful hymn full of optimism and belief that one day this picture of peace will be revealed. Our mission work together in Nicaragua is as close as we have come to realizing the meaning of this song. I will always remember when Gene, Roger and Sonia Gonzalez's family came to Hartsville, South Carolina. We sang this song while the Nicaraguan family talked around our dinner table. I watched Gene play and sing as we listened to them talking and laughing. "Have you seen the picture colored in Love?"

Song 13

I've see a picture but it's not in a book
And you will not find it so don't bother to look.
It's a picture of color It's a picture of peace.
It's world never ending It's a heavenly feast.
And I know that I've seen it, Though it's not very clear.
It's a vision I cherish that I'll always hold near
It's a world full of children and they never will die
From war or from hunger or some other lie.

It's a picture of all arms open to everyone
With hands tied to plowshares instead of a gun.
And theres only one heart and there's nothing to hide.
There's only one circle with the whole world inside
And the people are singing songs from every land.

Though the language is different you can still understand
And there's laughing and dancing, what a beautiful sight.
It's all in this picture, this picture of light.

Now I've seen a picture of a world in the sun.
All people together, standing as one.
Loving each other in the light hand in hand.
While the walls that divide us no longer stand.
Bring us together, shine down from above,
Paint us a picture with the color of love
With hope for tomorrow, show us the way,
Give us this picture, Give us this day.
Have you seen the picture colored with love?

I always dreamed
Id own a castle and be a King
But dreams arent what they always see
So the Pauper sings His song

And the fairytale fades away
As the magic spell seems to say
Youre set to sail to a humble
hide away...not far away

Chords

The Pauper is a King
If you erase the price of things
For within the King the pauper
finally found

That the truth of royalty rings
Within the very dream
Of the King who made a
broken heart His crown.

"Pauper and the King," 1984.
Original handwritten lyrics.

51

THE PAUPER AND THE KING

Before a downfall the heart is haughty, but humility comes before honor.
PROVERBS 18:12, NIV

Songs are like your children. This child is one of my favorites because it holds the essence of humility and servanthood. In a very simple way, it brings to light the beauty and power of brokenness. In just a few lines it reveals the royalty of what really matters in this world. On a side-note, my fascination with the Wizard of Oz spills over in the metaphor of "the pieces and the parts of broken hearts" becoming a crown. I still believe that the image I was searching for came directly from the Cowardly Lion who broke the vase in one of the movie scenes and placed it on his head as a crown. I always loved the thought of a crown being made of something broken and ordinary. I wrote this song in 1984.

Song 14

Well, I've always dreamed I'd own a castle and be a king

But dreams aren't what they always seem

So the pauper sings his song...on and on

And the fairytale fades away as the magic spell seems to say

You're set to sail to another place not so far away

Now the pauper is a king if you erase the price of things

For within the king the pauper finally found

That the truth of royalty rings within the very dream

Of a king who made a broken heart his crown

Now there was a king that lived within the very dream

Of making royalty out of broken things

And the pieces and the parts of broken hearts

He built His kingdom with

And He told the pauper if he would give his life to Him

That he could live as a king forevermore.

"In the Hands of God" album photo.

52

THE BEST OF FRIENDS

Greater love has no one than this: to lay down one's life for one's friends.
JOHN 15:13, NIV

"Heart of Love" was the name of our band. For over ten years, we ministered through music throughout the southeast. The band was made up of a group of guys from Charleston Southern University who had a common love for God and music. It was a family in the real sense of the word. Over thirty people were associated with our ministry during that period of time. It is hard to explain how close we became during those years. Night after night of concerts, small churches to large concert halls, we watched kids cry in our arms as they surrendered their lives to Christ. This song was written in 1988 as I anticipated our band coming to an end. It was a painful thought after all the miles, concerts, and truly incredible experiences of worship and sacrifice we'd shared. This was my way of saying goodbye to my best friends in the world.

Song 15

Do you remember the times we use to spend

Playing our music, praying God use it?

Thought it would never end

But from here I fear I'll never hold again

All of the times we left behind

We were the best of friends

But time will never change

And dreams can't rearrange

The love you find again and again

Will bring you back the best of friends

The best of friends will never say goodbye

Oh don't you cry, look into my eyes, you can depend

On the best of friends...they never really ever go away

They somehow stay until the end
And even then, we're the best of friends
You came for a moment and then you went away
But you're back to stay by your Spirit until the day
When you'll come again and from the sky you will descend
And then face to face we'll finally see the best of friends

53

LONLEY WORLD

Suppose one of you has a hundred sheep and loses one of them. Doesn't he leave the ninety-nine in the open country and go after the lost sheep until he finds it? And when he finds it, he joyfully puts it on his shoulders and goes home. Then he calls his friends and neighbors together and says, 'Rejoice with me; I have found my lost sheep.' I tell you that in the same way there will be more rejoicing in heaven over one sinner who repents than over ninety-nine righteous persons who do not need to repent.
Luke 15:4-7, NIV

"Lonely World" is a song I wrote in a hotel room in Orangeburg, South Carolina in 1985. It was a vision in my mind of a world living outside the security of God's love. It is a song that is "crying out" for someone to tell them about the love of God. The band sang this song every night for years in concert. It's the first of a two-song set that ended with "Midnight in the City." These two songs were not written together but complimented each other as one piece. It is a succession of questions ending with, "Who's going to tell them?"

Song 16

Can't you hear their silent screams,

Hardened hearts, and drunken dreams?

Can't you hear them crying out from the boulevard tonight?

Can't you hear them crying out?

Can't you hear their lonely shouts?

Can't you hear their dying doubts tonight?

Can't you hear them, crying, crying out?

Lost and lonely people wondering what life's about

Dying, hopeless boys and girls

Living while they die,

Dying in a lonely world

Sometimes we live so comfortably

That we don't take the time to see
The ultimate urgency in sharing Jesus' love.
How can we hesitate? How can we sit and wait?
Don't you know one day soon it will be too late...be too late.
Who's going to tell them?
Tell them about Jesus. He can free us.
Who's going to tell them?
Tell them about Jesus. He can free us.
Who's going to tell them?

54

MIDNIGHT IN THE CITY

Then I saw a new heaven and a new earth, for the first heaven and the first earth had passed away, and there was no longer any sea.
Revelation 21:1, NIV

I remember sitting on my bed in my college dorm room writing this song late at night in 1983. It was a vision of a torn and hurting world awaiting the coming of Christ. It is a picture of that glorious day when all the pain and strife will be wiped away. No matter how bad it gets on this earth; there will be a day when the clouds will open wide and Jesus will come back to take those who love Him to Heaven. He is coming back again.

Song 17

It's midnight in the city and darkness in the air
The street lights serenade the night with glimpses of despair.
They quietly uncover a drunkard in the street
And bar rooms flash their neon lights to everyone they meet,
But He's coming back again.
Fifty Second Avenue is quiet and all alone
People are sleeping in the silence of their homes.
As Daddy worked the night shift the little children dream,
And leaping in my silence I heard a lady scream,
But He's coming back again.
Somewhere on the front page the morning paper read
Young boy in an alleyway from an overdose is dead.
Somewhere on the back page said a baby lost his home
Lying in a trash can dying all alone,
But He's coming back again.

55

IT'S ALL RIGHT

For the love of money is a root of all kinds of evil. Some people, eager for money, have wandered from the faith and pierced themselves with many griefs.
I TIMOTHY 6:10, NIV

This song wrote itself back in the summer of 1983. It centered around a message about money and the free gift of Christ. The imagery portrays the free gift of nature in the first verse. Then, I move to the humorous and useless struggle with money in the second verse. Last, I say that I would rather be poor and sing than be the richest man on Earth. The chorus says, "Its All Right" because everything we ever really wanted—God's love—is free.

Song 18

Honeysuckle smell is swarming on an easy Sunday morning

A weeping willow dancing to the tune the wind is playing

The sunshine peeks through the pines

A southern symphony

From the loft the swaying singers listen to the breeze

And It's All right...It's All right...It's All right

Life is All right with me

Cause Life is Jesus

And His love is free

My life is full of thoughtless laughter

Looking at the morning after

'Cause life is but a one act play... a penniless parade

Of passing by those trees of green

Invisible charade of pleas

The monetary masquerade can sink into the seas.

I'd rather be a poor man on God's earth to sing a song
'Cause there is life in music
When it is your master's home
And I'd still be hung and struggling within the needle's eye
If I'd held on to the roots of trees that grow so high.

When I was young I thought
the Summer last fore
I'd sail the Stormy weather

All Alone

All on my Own

I stood the test of time
And left behind what mattered
Now my life is shattered scattered
in the silence of the song

on In just a void man
And til time I've hads gone by
the I'd give the sun a setting

As I shed a tear and
cry
cry
All on my Own

Enough I had a
Second chances
To live my life in not
romance
Not just another song
not chance
alone
OUT

"All on My Own," 1988.
Original handwritten lyrics.

56

ALL ON MY OWN

Not that we are competent in ourselves to claim anything for ourselves,
but our competence comes from God.
2 CORINTHIANS 3:5, NIV

"All on My Own" is another one of my favorite songs from my own backyard.
I wrote this song in 1988 in the storage room attached to the townhouse in
Summerville, South Carolina. It was the first home Debra and I purchased
after living in a trailer for a few years following college. I found myself
sitting at the piano imagining the seasons of a man's life; a man who
decided to live in the self-sufficiency of his own power and pride. He was
a young man running wild without a thought of God. Then he moved
through college, work, and family without a prayer. Finally, as an old man he
reflected on all that had happened, all on his own. It is a sad commentary on
the existence of so many people. They wait 'til the last minute to place their
lives in the hands of God. Though heartbreaking, I thank God for the gift of
this song in communicating the choice to live without Him—
All on my own.

Song 19

When I was young I always thought the sun would last forever

I'd sail through stormy weather all alone

All on my own

I stood the test of time and left behind the things that matter

Shattered pieces scattered in a song

All on my own

All on my own, I thought I'd find the reason

For the changing of the seasons in my soul

But I was wrong

To live my life without You

On my own.

Just a kid who finished college in the autumn of my youth

By the springtime all my knowledge had killed the seed of truth
All on my own.
I made a life so full of strife I bought a home, forgot my wife
The kids are gone without a prayer
All on my own.
I always thought tomorrow would bring another day
When I would fall upon my knees and pray,
But now with only memories I can honestly say
That tomorrow was today.
Now I'm just an old man and time has passed me by
As I stare into the mirror I can't find a reason why
On my own.
I watch the sun set upon the dead of winter sky
As I hang my head and cry I guess I'll have to die
All on my own.

Early in the Evening   Late in Autumn
I saw the Wind blowing in the trees
And I watched the leaves go dancing through
                the columns
Riding on the backseat of a breeze

Bouncing like the children on a playground
I watched the silence quietly call their na
And they'd twirl awhile until they landed on
                the front porch
And then sat still til the Wind would blow ag

And love is Always .... Dancing in the Wind

I watched an eagle fly into the mountains
And I wondered how it felt to be so fre
Then closed my eyes and took a ride to Some
To try and find that the deepest part of me

When I got there I saw an old man sailin
Out upon an open stormy Everlasting sea
But He only raised His sail when the wind
And he found His destination like the leave
                on His Knees

Love is always .... Dancing in the Wind

"Dancing in the Wind," 1987.
Original handwritten lyrics.

57

DANCING IN THE WIND

When the day of Pentecost came, they were all together in one place.
Suddenly a sound like the blowing of a violent wind came from heaven and
filled the whole house where they were sitting.
ACTS 2:1 NIV

It was a moment I will never forget. One of those perfect autumn nights I carried my guitar outside on to the porch to seek inspiration. The wind was blowing through the trees while my dog Puddles was sleeping at my feet. As I sat playing my guitar, a leaf blew off the tree, danced around in the wind, and landed on the front porch. I watched the leaf settle down as the wind subsided, only to wait for the wind to reappear, and carry it up in the air to land once again. That leaf represents our lives. We sit still until the unseen wind of God's Spirit moves us to our destination. Love is always "Dancing in the Wind." When I finished writing this song, I reached down and picked up the leaf that inspired me and placed it inside my guitar. That leaf is still there. Every time I begin to play, that leaf rustles around, and the sound transports me to that moment in 1987 when God spoke to my heart about the power of His Spirit in our lives.

Song 20

It was early in the evening and late in the autumn
When I saw the wind go blowing through the trees,
And I watched the leaves go dancing through the columns
Riding on the backseat of a breeze.
Bouncing like the children on a playground
I watched the silence quietly call their names,
And they twirled around until they landed down on the front porch
And they sat there until the wind would call again.
Love is always...Dancing in the Wind

I saw an eagle fly into the mountains
And I wondered how it felt to be so free,
So I closed my eyes and I took a ride to nowhere
To see the very deepest part of me.
There I saw an old man on the ocean
He was sailing on an everlasting sea,
But he only raised his sails when the wind was blowing
And he found his destination like the leaves.
Love is always...Dancing in the Wind

Sometimes my prayers are like those friendly dancers,
I have no answers and I don't know which way to go,
So why should I take chances on the ocean
'Cause only God knows where the wind will blow.
So like the leaves I want no destination,
I'll just let the wind come and take me home,
And there I'll see that old man on the ocean,
And he'll say, "Boy, I'd never made it on my own."
Love is always...Dancing in the Wind

THE OLD DESERTED ALTAR

I SEE A TIME A COMIN
WHEN OUR CHILDREN DO NOT SEE
A NEED TO BOW AND WORSHIP HIM
UPON THEIR BENDED KNEE

AND THEY'll FORGET THAT SUNDAY MORNING
WAS A TIME TO PRAISE HIS NAME
AND WHEN THE CHURCHES FALL—
THEIR STEEPLES TALL
WILL TUMBLE DOWN THE SAME

AND THERE WITHIN THE RUINS
IS AN ALTAR STANDING TALL
PROCLAIMING THAT THE LORD OF HOST
IS STILL OUR ALL AND ALL

THE OLD DESERTED ALTAR WAITS PATIENTLY
FOR YOU AND ME ON BENDED KNEE TO BOW BE
THRONE
AND PRAY FOR OUR DESIRE TO BURN LIKE FIRE
THE OLD DESERTED ALTAR WILL STAND UNTIL

"The Old Deserted Alter," 1987.
Original handwritten lyrics.

58

THE OLD DESERTED ALTAR

The Lord appeared to Abram and said, "To your offspring I will give this land."
So he built an altar there to the Lord, who had appeared to him.
GENESIS 12:7, NIV

In 1987, I envisioned an "Old Deserted Altar" standing in the midst of a church that was empty and falling down in ruins. I imagined a day in our future when our churches are empty and young people do not see a need to bow and worship Him upon their bended knee. But then I heard a strong ever-present voice within my heart that said, "I will remain." There will always be a place where man can surrender to God's love, with or without a building. If everything falls, the "Old Deserted Altar" will stand as an everlasting symbol of God's holiness and love. Catherine Booth once said, "I would rather die than lower the standard of God's righteousness." The world may move away from God, but God will never leave us or forsake us. The altar is a constant reminder of a sacred place where sinful man can meet a holy and just God. "The Old Deserted Altar will stand until the end."

Song 21

Well, I see a time a coming

When our children will not see

A need to bow and worship Him

Upon their bended knees

And they'll forget that Sunday morning

Was a time to praise His name

When the churches fall, the steeples tall

Will tumble down the same.

But there within the ruins

Is an altar standing tall

Professing that the Lord of host

Is still our all in all.

The Old Deserted Altar
Waits patiently alone
For you and me on bended knee
To bow before the throne
And pray that our desire will burn like fire again.
The Old Deserted Altar
Will stand until the end.

There's another day not far away
On a still and silent night
When the Old Deserted Altar will be standing in a light
That will shine down out of heaven
As the clouds will open wide
And the few found at the altar

Will then begin to rise.
Every knee shall bow and every tongue confess
That Jesus Christ is Lord of all
And our self -righteousness
Will sink into the distant past,
For at last that day we'll see
That the Old Deserted Altar was the only place to be.

59

MIRACLES

*Keep watch over yourselves and all the flock of which the Holy Spirit
has made you overseers. Be shepherds of the church of God,
which He bought with His own blood.*
ACTS 20:28, NIV

This song was written as a response to our growing fascination with
miracles. It seems that Christendom has regressed in this age to an
obsession with entertainment instead of true faith. I began to pray and think
about the need for God's people not to seek the glitter and glamor of some
television ministry, but the miracle of God still loving us. The fact that God
loved us and gave His life for us is the only miracle we really need. Instead
of searching for a "magician in a shiny traveling show," look at my life in
the light of God's mercy and grace. "I am the greatest miracle that the world
could ever hope to see. It was when a holy God in heaven loved a lowly
sinner such as me."

Song 22

Everybody's looking for a miracle
Like God is some magician in a shiny traveling show.
People come from miles around
To see the latest sights and sounds
But they don't understand or even know

That You are more than earthly miracles.
You're deeper than the things we say and do
But I believe I saw the greatest miracle
The day I saw the love for me found in the heart of You.

And I am the greatest miracle
That the world could ever hope to see.
It was when a holy God in heaven above
Loved a lowly sinner such as me.

I am the greatest miracle
And I believe I saw the perfect way.
It was when a holy God in heaven above
Loved me enough to stay.

So if you're looking for a miracle
You don't have to search so far to see
That by His Grace He chose to stay.
He didn't turn and run away
And made the greatest miracle of me.

"Love Won't Leave You Lonely," album cover.

60

LOVE WON'T LEAVE YOU LONELY

Never will I leave you; never will I forsake you.
HEBREWS 13:5, NIV

The word lonely is woven within the fabric of my musical expression. I did not plan it that way; but lonely emerges as a constant theme in the body of my message. This song is the title of my second album. I wrote it in my garage office in Hartsville, South Carolina, in 1997. I believe that loneliness is a human being's greatest fear. This song says that no matter the circumstance, "Love Won't Leave You Lonely."

Song 23

So many times before love has walked right out the door
Left you standing, crying in the rain
So when you stare into the sky and the tears flow from your eyes
And you ask God why you have to stand this pain

Hold on until tomorrow because I promise you
Love will see you through.

Love won't leave you lonely,
It will last until the end.
And long lost friend, if you're the only
One left alone you can depend
That Love won't leave you lonely

There's an everlasting Love that shines down from above
This Love I'm speaking of will never die,
So when you're feeling all alone left out on your own
Remember Love is waiting...anticipating
That one day you'll find your way back home.

61

THE CITY OF ABANDONED DREAMS

The angel of God said to me in a dream, 'Jacob'. I answered, "Here I am."
GENESIS 31:11, NIV

Dreams are the lifeblood of the soul. Like the Scripture says, "A people without a vision die." This song is a vision of a city where people go when they abandon their dreams. "It's a lonely place…I can't describe…a place where people run and hide and they leave their hearts in the grave beside—The City of Abandoned Dreams." Why do we bury our dreams? There is such light and life in the dreams of God's love. Fear kills our belief in things unseen and we slowly allow these doubts to steal away our desire to make the world a better place. Fear hardens our hearts and leads us to surrender to a cold and hopeless world. So many throw away their talents and let fear render their lives useless and dead. This song is a battle cry to believe in dreams and to believe in the power of holy imagination. God is ready and able to empower our dreams. I wrote this song in 1995 in the garage/office in Hartsville, South Carolina. We must dream and allow God to work through us to change the world.

Song 24

There's a loneliness I can't describe,
A place where people go and hide
And they leave their hearts in the grave beside
The city of abandoned dreams

I pity all the lonely fools
That never used their talents as tools
Useless lives they live or so it seems
In the city of abandoned dreams

They never thought they could change the world
So they laid down and died with their flags left unfurled

They never dreamed that the lives they lead
Would unveil the peace the whole world needs.
They never bleed for the lonely ones
Who are dying in the streets.
But they stand in their halls, stare at the walls,
Justify why church bells ring.
It's a lonely place
In the city of abandoned dreams

They hesitate, they sit and wait.
They let their love grow cold to hate,
And they kill their own and run for home
In the city of abandoned dreams.

So still they sit, they mock, they spit.
They cast their lots into the pits
In the name of Love, they still push and shove
In the city of abandoned dreams

62

GIVE LOVE TIME

For the revelation awaits an appointed time; it speaks of the end and will not prove false. Though it linger, wait for it; it will certainly come and will not delay.
HABAKKUK 2:3, NIV

All my life, I have heard the old saying that "time can heal a broken heart." But the longer I live, the less I believe it. How do broken hearts get fixed? I believe that love is the only thing that can mend our brokenness. God is love, and if you give love time, love will find a way.

Song 25

Walking around with your heart on the ground
Wondering when things are going to change.
In a matter of time all the reason and rhyme
Will come alive and light your way.

Time won't heal a broken heart
No matter what people say.
Time won't heal a broken heart.
Give Love time, Love will find a way.

Sometimes we act like we own time
When we ask Him to heal our pain.
We say, "Hey, Time, old friend, won't you come on and send
Me some shelter from the rain?"

If you give Love time He will heal your mind,
Find all the missing parts
Of a life that was shattered.
Though the pieces are scattered

Love will mend your broken heart.
Oh and Love will mend a broken heart,
No matter what people say.
Love will mend a broken heart
If you give Love time
Love will find a way.

Tina and Ryan Kauffmann. The song "From Here" was written and dedicated to her courageous and inspiring life.
Born at Table 7 - Tulane University 2006.

63

FROM HERE

For this reason I kneel before the Father, from whom every family in heaven and on earth derives its name. I pray that out of His glorious riches He may strengthen you with power through His Spirit in your inner being, so that Christ may dwell in your hearts through faith. And I pray that you, being rooted and established in love, may have power, together with all the Lord's holy people, to grasp how wide and long and high and deep is the love of Christ, and to know this love that surpasses knowledge—that you may be filled to the measure of all the fullness of God.

Now to Him who is able to do immeasurably more than all we ask or imagine, according to His power that is at work within us
EPHESIANS 3:14-20, NIV

I have worked in higher education for my entire career. For over 25 years, I have been associated with CASE (Council for Advancement and Support of Education) and through this organization I have made many long-standing friendships. This song is dedicated to one of those "one in a million" friends. Her name is Tina Kauffmann, and this is her story and song. Tina had been living with a kidney transplant for nearly ten years when this song was written. Because of my experience with my father's heart transplant, we shared a very strong understanding and connection through the years. I always felt a deep empathy for Tina and played the role of "protector" on our frequent trips across the Southeast. I felt that her husband would appreciate someone who really understood her situation when she was so far away. So I accepted the privilege of making sure Tina had someone to call on if she needed anything.

Our conversations about the meaning of faith and the brevity of life carried us to a depth of friendship that few people share in life. Through the years, our extended conversations grew a strong and sturdy appreciation and respect. I was inspired by Tina's positive attitude on life and her relentless desire to meet challenges head on. She is an extraordinary individual who elevates everything around her.

One weekend in 2006 our travels with CASE took us to New Orleans. During dinner with some colleagues at Tulane University, we were talking about the importance of living life to its fullest and never taking a moment for granted. I asked Tina if she had heard the song by Tim McGraw "Live Like You are Dying" She said she had not, so I began to sing the song at the dinner table. To my surprise, the rest of our friends started singing with me. There we were singing the chorus together...

At the end of the song, after the laughter subsided, Tina looked at me and said, "Wouldn't it be great if everyone lived this way all the time from their heart? 'From Here' life looks so much more precious. What if everyone lived 'From Here—from their heart's every moment of life?'"

That statement inspired me to write a song that invites others to live "From Here." That song was sung for the first time when we did a concert for *Legacy Road*. Tina was right there on stage. It was an unforgettable moment.

Song 26

From Here...I can see forever

From Here, All my dreams come true

From Here, Whatever the weather

The Sun comes shining through, it's true.

From Here, the night turns into morning

From Here, the darkness disappears

From Here, the light is shining brighter

And the sun is warm and near, it's clear

From Here

From Here is not a far and distant place, not an uphill race,

not a far and distant shore

Here... Here is in your heart and that's the place to start to find what love is for

From Here

From Here, I hear the children singing

From Here, a song of hope and love

From Here, the world joins in the chorus

And we all can sing as One, as One

From Here

"Legacy Road: The Dream Lives On," logo.

64

RIVER OF MERCY

*But from everlasting to everlasting the Lord's love is with those who fear him,
and his righteousness with their children's children—with those who keep
his covenant and remember to obey his precepts.*
PSALM 103:17-18, NIV

"River of Mercy" is one of those songs I started in 1998 and then finished 10 years later in April 2008. Interestingly, God sometimes teaches you through a song and then lets you finish it after the lessons are learned. God allowed me to finish this song right when I needed His mercy the most. The day I finished it, I saw the mercy of God more clearly than ever before. This song starts in a dreary state looking for the mercy of God and ends with a ship that's coming to carry me home. That's the way God works. So if you are lost and lonely, remember, there is a ship on the way to carry you to a place of mercy and peace. Your love is like a river of mercy...

Song 27

Woke up this morning
Feeling kind of blue.
Don't know where I'm going
Or what I'm going to do.
So lost and lonely Lord
And looking for a way
To the river of mercy
To Your love in the bay.
So I keep on growing stronger everyday,
Looking for that distant shore
Trying to find my way.

(Chorus)
Your love is like a river of mercy
Leading me down to the ocean of love
Your love is like a river of mercy
Leading me down to the ocean of love

Waiting and watching
Just beyond the sun
My day is over Lord before it has begun.
I get so weary but I keep hanging on
'Cause I know that there's a ship to sail
And carry me back home.

(Chorus)

(Bridge)
And so I keep on flowing toward the ocean.
Just a matter of time
Until I find myself at the mercy of the motion
Leading me to Your loving kindness.

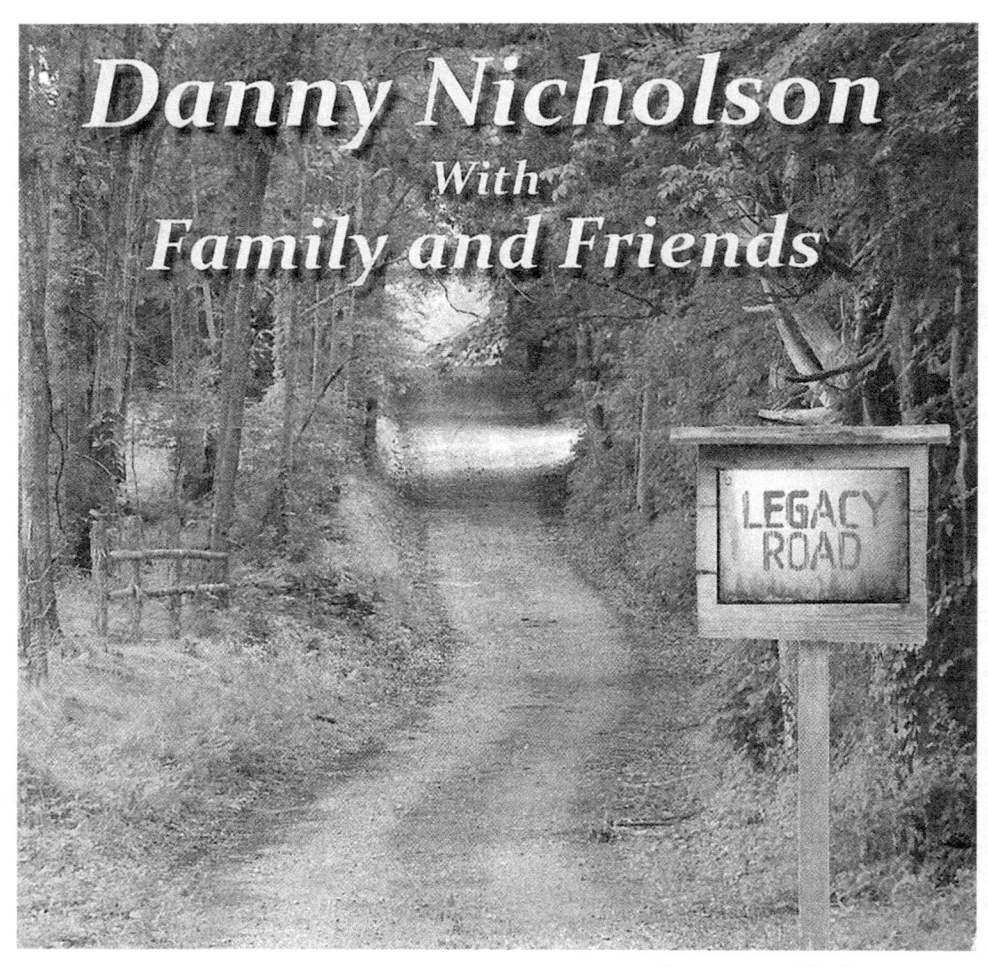

"Legacy Road," album cover.

65

ASHES TO GLORY

*...and provide for those who grieve in Zion—to bestow on them a crown of beauty
instead of ashes, the oil of joy instead of mourning, and a garment of praise
instead of a spirit of despair. They will be called oaks of righteousness,
a planting of the Lord for the display of his splendor.*
ISAIAH 61:3, NIV

I wrote "Ashes to Glory" for our fourth album, "Legacy Road." The album
was a compilation of songs about family, faith, and friends offered by
my best friends to raise money for the children of Nicaragua. The song
references a very tough time in my life when I felt like everything was
burned down and left to die. God has a way of turning ashes into His glory
and this song captured the hope I have in God to make all things work for
the good of those called according to His purpose.

Song 28

*Burn it down to the ground
And watch it rise back up again*

*Foolish pride will bring you down
To a place you've never been*

*You will fly to the sky
When you're ready to ascend*

And the ashes will turn to glory once again.

*They flew those planes into the buildings
They fell down like waters flow*

*To the ground so the people
In their hearts would always know*

That the ruins of a nation,
Will come alive in the end
And the ashes will turn to glory once again.

Oh, the dreams of a nation
Oh, the life of just one soul

Has to die to begin,
Then the ashes will turn to glory once again

**Jeff Francisco and Nicholson at the Connie Maxwell farm
during the "New Beginnings" Celebration.**
Photo: Kevin Jones

Last Words

IT'S ALL THAT'S LEFT TO YOU

Jesus said, "It is finished." With that, he bowed his head and gave up his spirit.
JOHN 19:30, NIV

You've probably heard the saying, "Home is where the heart is."

As I write this final chapter, I think it would be good for us to think deeply about what backyard really means. During my attempt in this book to reveal my own backyard, I have shared in many different ways a working definition of backyard for me. Backyard is "a special place behind my home." Think about that thought with me for a moment.

My own backyard is the place where I was born and raised, the cocoon where my imagination was nurtured, the grassy patch where I laid my head down and dreamed, the cradle for my first tree house, the place where I heard the sound of my mother's voice calling me for dinner, the church where I had conversations with God, the painted canvas of every tree, flower, butterfly, dandelion, and bird that I heard sing outside my bedroom window, the ball field where I threw my first baseball to dad, and the scrapbook of my summer time memories. Yes, all of these images and more remind me of my own backyard, a special place behind my heart.

As I look over my shoulder and see the last fifty years etched on these pages, I relive the stories, hear the songs, and feel the Spirit speak to me about my own backyard, a special place behind my home. You see, it really all started right there in the innocence of my childhood and, just like Dorothy said in my favorite scene of the movie, *The Wizard of Oz,*

> "I learned that if I ever go looking for happiness again, I won't have to look any further than my own backyard. Because if it isn't there, I never really lost it to begin with."

This book is my life story but it is really more than that. It is your life story. How? Well, I have found that we as human beings are pretty much all the same. We are spring- loaded to wander beyond that special place behind our home. We find ourselves searching in a lost and lonely world for a place like

Oz that will meet our most cherished desires and lofty dreams only to find in the end that it was back in Kansas the whole time. My hope and prayer is that you will begin and end by finding happiness in your own backyard and by realizing that you don't have to go far to find that happiness is right behind your home.

All the stories in this book in some way or another are trying to say this one thing. Whether it's my son finding God in the stars, a glimpse of Heaven with a Silver Spoon, an old man carving a guitar out of a tree, my dad getting a new heart, the reason behind my son's name, a conversation just beyond the fence, the journal of *Legacy Road* or the Heart of Boston, all roads have led to that special place behind my heart. The songs, the poems, every step of the journey has brought me closer and closer to where I started from in the beginning.

So now I struggle to say goodbye. Goodbyes are hard. They always have been and the end of this book is no different. How does one say goodbye in the final chapter? Well, come to think of it, I already have. You see, we live forever through what we leave behind our heart. Our stories, poems, songs, children, grandchildren, and memories of those who we loved along the way define our legacy. This is my legacy. No, I am not famous and won't ever make a million dollars. My face will never be plastered across the front pages of glamor magazines. The bright lights of the camera will not flash across the red carpet of my life and in a way, I found true happiness by avoiding the world's attempt to define my happiness. As full as my life has been, it is a kind of quiet goodbye in the context of fame and fortune. I chose the road less traveled. I chose substance instead of form. I intentionally surrendered to the fact that life was not a parade of glitter and empty applause but a simple circle of family and friends gathered around the campfire of faith, mission, and meaning. If you haven't noticed yet that doesn't sell in this old world and like many of my heroes mentioned in these pages, it is the defining decision in one's life. What is said about me will come and go, but what is left behind my heart will last forever. Lasting stuff matters and in the end that is my legacy and indeed the content of my final words to you.

The last question is this—What will you leave in that special place behind your heart? What is your legacy? Will you find yourself empty-handed at the end of the road? Or will you find yourself surrounded by faith, family and friends sharing the meaning and truth of a life well-lived?

The lights go out, the stage is silent, the seats are empty and nothing is left but the memory of your story written in some dusty book sitting on your son's bookshelf. Is that enough? Will you even be remembered? Oh, I think so. On some quiet night when everyone is sleeping, my grandson will open the pages of this book and yearn to know where he came from. And what will he find? The truth dressed in stories about his dad, granddad, and the many holy moments simply buried in the sound of three chords and a few poetic words. He will close the pages, cut off the lights, and sit in the darkness. I watch him slowly bow his head and pray. My hopes and dreams will then be accomplished. For you see, I wrote this book especially for him and for every other human being who seeks to find happiness in their own backyard.

Goodbye. Don't forget to keep the porch light on until I make it home and be sure to look over your shoulder every time you pull out the drive way because, there in your own backyard you will remember the reason for your brief visit. The memories will dance like visions of grace and whisper in your heart's ear, "There is no place like home."

Embrace that moment my friend. It's all that's left to you.

Hold fast to dreams
For if dreams die
Life is a broken winged bird that can not fly
Hold fast to dreams
For if dreams go
Life is a frozen field covered with snow.

- Langston Hughes

MY OWN
backyard

MY OWN
backyard

CPSIA information can be obtained
at www.ICGtesting.com
Printed in the USA
LVHW040609150119
603922LV00001B/1/P